The Cutworm Moths of Ontario and Quebec

Eric W. Rockburne
and
J. Donald Lafontaine
Biosystematics Research Institute
Ottawa, Ontario

Photographs by
Thomas H. Stovell

Research Branch
Canada Department of Agriculture
Publication 1593 1976

© Minister of Supply and Services Canada 1976

Available by mail from

Printing and Publishing
Supply and Services Canada
Ottawa, Canada K1A 0S9

or through your bookseller.

Catalogue No. A43-1593/1976   Price: Canada: $ 8.50
ISBN 0-660-00514-X   Other countries: $10.20

Price subject to change without notice.

The Cutworm Moths
of Ontario and Quebec

INTRODUCTION

The cutworm, or owlet, moths constitute a family belonging to the order Lepidoptera. This order consists of all the moths and butterflies. Cutworm moths are common throughout the world. In Canada and the United States over three thousand species are represented, from the Arctic tundra to the arid deserts of southwestern United States. Many species are found in eastern North America, but the family is best represented in the mountains and on the plateaus of western North America.

CLASSIFICATION AND NOMENCLATURE

In zoology, classification is the systematic arrangement of animals into related groups and categories, and nomenclature is the system of names given to these groups.

The cutworm moths are insects that belong in the class Insecta. Insecta is divided into several orders: Diptera, the true flies; Hymenoptera, the wasps, bees, and ants; Coleoptera, the beetles; and so on. The order Lepidoptera includes all the moths and butterflies. Each order is divided into a number of families, and the Noctuidae family, which includes all the cutworm moths, is a family of the Lepidoptera. Based on apparently naturally related groups, some families are divided into subfamilies. Groups of closely related species within a family or subfamily are called genera (singular, genus). The basic unit in classification is the species (singular and plural). A species may be defined as a group of intimately related and physically similar individuals that potentially or actually interbreed. When the generic and specific names are written out, they should be underlined, or printed in italics. The generic name is always written with an initial capital letter and the specific name in lowercase letters. The specific name is usually followed by the name of the person who first described the species and proposed its name; this person is called the author of the species.

The classification of a typical cutworm moth, the black cutworm, is as follows:

Animal Kingdom
    Phylum Arthropoda (animals with a segmented exoskeleton)
        Class Insecta (insects)
            Order Lepidoptera (moths and butterflies)
                Family Noctuidae (cutworm moths)
                    Subfamily Noctuinae
                        Agrotis ipsilon (Hufnagel)
                        (genus) (species) (author)

LIFE HISTORY AND HABITS

Most cutworm moths are nocturnal and are active only during the hours of darkness. However, a few species in the family are adjusted to daylight, or diurnal, activity. In one subfamily of the Noctuidae, the Heliothidinae, many species are diurnal or at least partly so.

Cutworm moths, like other moths and butterflies, have four distinct stages in their developmental cycle: egg; larva (plural, larvae) or caterpillar; pupa (plural, pupae); and adult. The eggs vary in shape from species to species: spherical, oval, conical, or pancake-shaped. The number of eggs laid also varies. The female of one species may lay only about a dozen eggs, whereas the female of another species may lay thousands. The eggs are deposited in various locations, depending mainly on the feeding habits of the larvae. The eggs of most true cutworms are laid in the soil, and those belonging to species that feed aboveground are usually laid on the leaves, twigs, or bark of their food plant. Some species remain in the egg stage for a long time, even over the winter, whereas other species remain in the egg stage for only a few days.

The young larva sometimes eats all or part of the shell it hatched from before it begins to feed on adjacent vegetation. During its larval stage, the insect molts several times, that is, it splits its old tight skin and emerges with a new looser one. The skin of a caterpillar has a limited elasticity and as the caterpillar matures the body becomes too big for the skin. A new skin and head capsule form under the old skin, before the old skin is shed. If development is not interrupted and the larva continues to feed, the insect may remain in the larval stage for only 10 days. However, the larval stage may last for several weeks.

At the completion of feeding, the larva either tunnels into the soil several inches deep and forms an oval cell, or spins a cocoon on the food plant or in the debris at the surface of the ground. Within a few days the larva gradually becomes inactive, and the pupa forms inside the last larval skin. The larval skin finally splits to expose the pupa, which is white at first, but gradually darkens, usually to dark brown.

The tissues within the pupa reorganize and the adult moth forms within the pupal skin. If development is not retarded, the insect may remain in the pupal stage for only a week or two.

The adult emerges from the pupal case by cracking the case along definite fracture lines on the ventral surface. If the pupa forms in a cocoon, the adult emerges from one end of the cocoon, but if the pupa forms in an earthen cell, the adult digs its way to the surface, probably through the channel formed by the larva when it was burrowing into the ground. The wings of the freshly emerged moth are small, soft, and padlike. When the adult reaches the surface of the ground or emerges from its cocoon, it climbs up on some object and rests quietly. The adult expands its wings by pumping blood into them. After the wings are fully formed and have dried, the insect is ready for flight. The moth may live from a few weeks to several months. Some moths overwinter as an adult. Moths feed only on liquids and may be found visiting flowers late in the evening. It is only the larva that damages plants by eating the foliage.

THE STRUCTURE OF A CUTWORM MOTH

The cutworm moths, like all insects, have three body divisions: head, thorax, and abdomen. The head bears a large compound eye on each side, a pair of feelers or antennae at the front, and a pair of feathery processes ventrally called the labial palps. The palps enclose between them the coiled tongue or proboscis, which is uncoiled to siphon up sweet liquids when the moth is feeding.

The thorax, the middle division of the body, bears three pairs of legs, the forelegs, the mid-legs, and the hind legs. The thorax also bears two pairs of wings, the fore wings and the hind wings. The wings of butterflies and moths are covered with minute scales that overlap like the shingles of a roof. The names used for the margins and angles of the wings are shown in the drawing. Among the cutworm moths, certain lines and spots are present on the wings of most species.

The last division of the body is the abdomen and it bears at its posterior end the external genitalia. The external genitalia, of both male and female, are often used in classifying and also in distinguishing the natural components of groups of closely related species.

Most cutworm moths are of medium size, varying in wing expanse from 1 to 2 inches (2 to 5 cm). However, some are much larger and others much smaller. The black witch, *Erebus odora* (Linnaeus), an occasional migrant into Canada from the south, has a wing expanse over 6 inches (15 cm). However, several species in the subfamily Acontiinae have wing expanses of only slightly more than one-quarter inch (6 mm). Cutworm moths usually have stout bodies covered with scales and hair.

Details of wings.

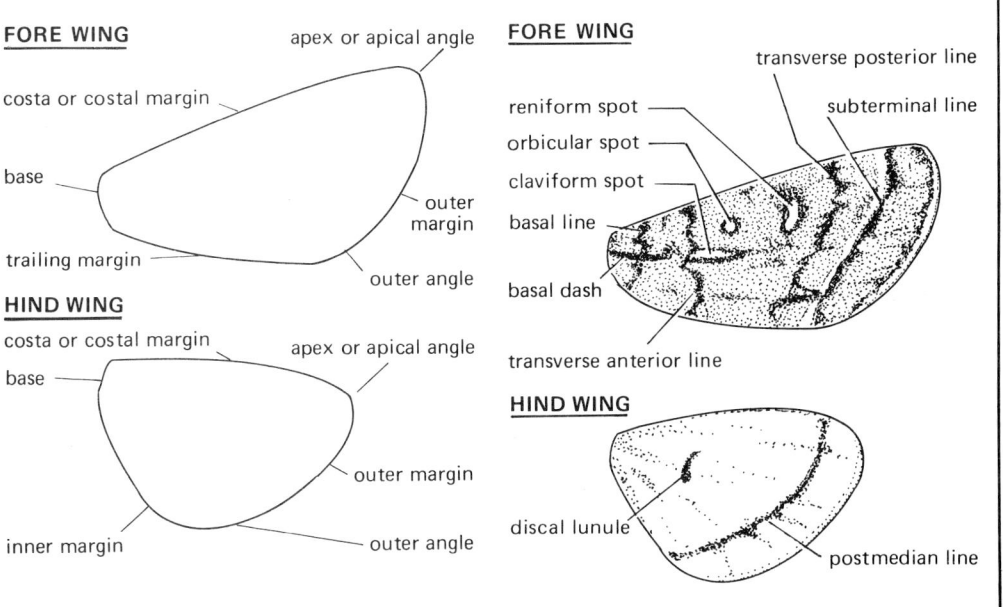

7

MAKING A COLLECTION OF CUTWORM MOTHS

Making a collection of cutworm moths can be a fascinating hobby, and your interest in the pastime will increase as you become more and more familiar with the species in your vicinity. Hard-bodied insects are maintained in collections by pinning them with insect pins and preserving them in a dried state. Moths and butterflies are pinned through the middle of the thorax, and the wings are spread out at right angles to the body on a specially designed spreading board and allowed to dry in this position. A small label indicating where the specimen was collected, the date, and the name of the collector should also be on the pin on which the specimen is mounted. Methods of collecting and preserving insects have been described in a publication compiled by B. P. Beirne entitled *Collecting, preparing, and preserving insects,* which may be obtained from the Publishing Centre of the Department of Supply and Services.

Because most cutworm moths are nocturnal, collecting at night with the aid of a light or by means of "sugaring" is the most productive. In the sugaring method, a mixture of beer and molasses or vinegar and brown sugar or some other sweet solution is painted on trees or fence posts, and these sites are later visited to collect the moths that have gathered. With the aid of a flashlight, you can flip the specimens you want into a killing bottle. Another method of obtaining good specimens is by collecting larvae and rearing them to the adult stage.

ORGANIZATION AND SCOPE OF THIS HANDBOOK

The arrangement of subfamilies, genera, and species in this handbook follows the arrangement in the Canadian National Collection (CNC) of Insects, which is in the custody of the Biosystematics Research Institute, Canada Department of Agriculture, Ottawa. All the species from Ontario and Quebec that are recorded in the CNC are illustrated. In some cases, the species in such groups are not well known taxonomically and confusion still exists regarding what components of the group represent valid species. In other cases, species of a group are well defined but cannot be distinguished except by reference to the genitalia or other microscopic structures.

This handbook is intended for the amateur. The photographs include all the cutworm moths occurring in Ontario and Quebec. To identify insects by examining the antennae, the veins in the wing, and the genitalia, you need to use a binocular microscope, which is beyond the budget of most amateurs. With practice, however, most individuals can develop a very good "eye" for distinguishing species.

Usually only one sex of each species is illustrated. It should be noted, however, that the hind wing of the female is usually somewhat darker than that of the male.

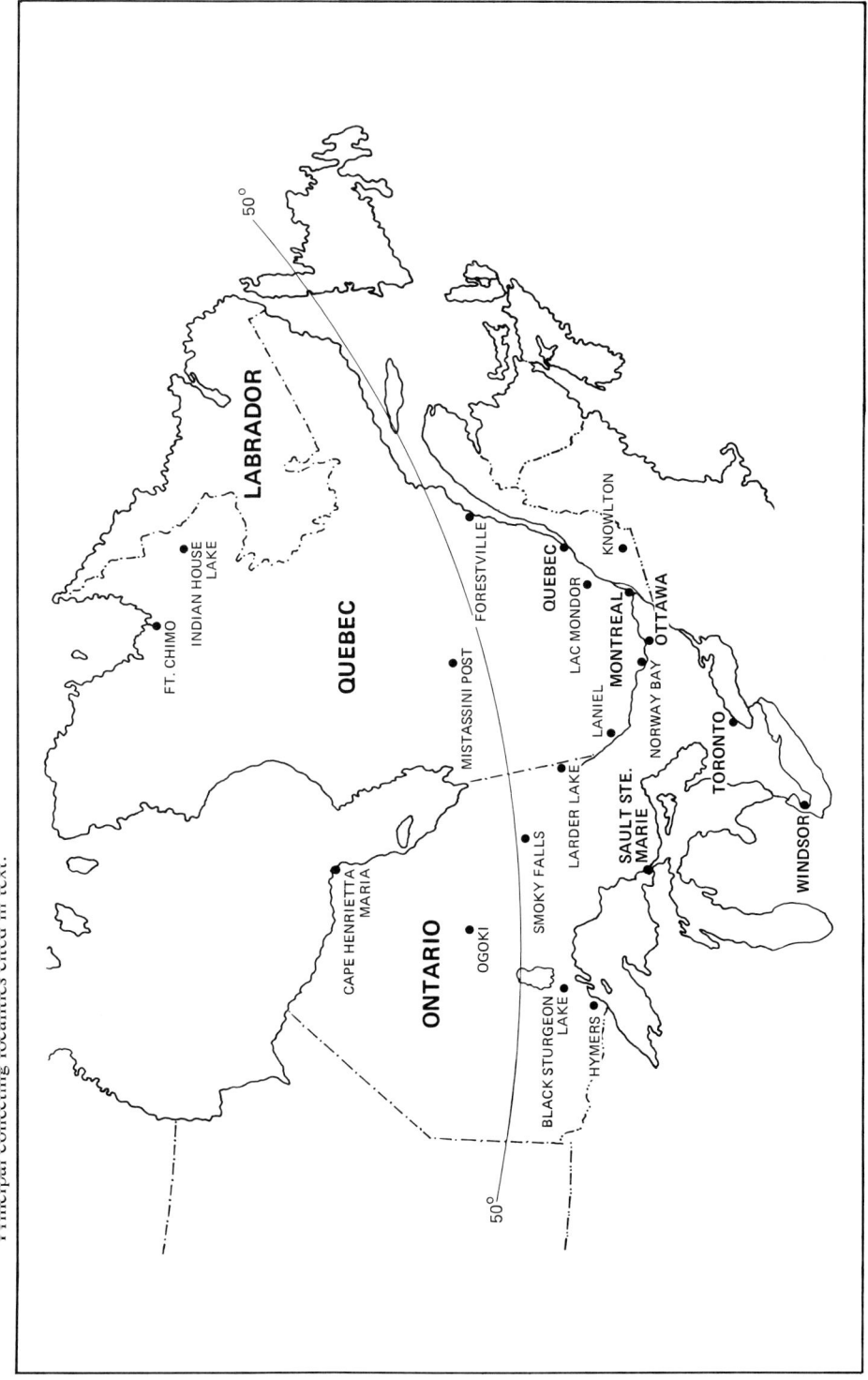

All specimens have been reproduced at natural size except for two species belonging in the subfamily Catocalinae, whose sizes are given in the explanation of the plate.

Host plants for the larvae are based on the rearing records of the Biosystematics Research Institute and on the Forest Insect Survey. The following references were helpful in the preparation of this publication:

Crumb, S.E. 1956. *The larvae of the Phalaenidae.* U.S. Dep. Agric. Tech. Bull. 1135.

Forbes, W.T.M. 1954. *Lepidoptera of New York and neighboring states. Part III. Noctuidae.* Cornell University, Agricultural Experiment Station, Ithaca, New York.

Can. Dep. Forest. 1962. *Forest Lepidoptera of Canada recorded by the Forest Insect Survey.* Vol. 2, Bull. 128.

FAMILY NOCTUIDAE
Subfamily Agaristinae

The subfamily consists of brightly colored, day-flying moths, which are usually found flitting near their food plant. The larvae are also brightly colored and, unlike most cutworm moth larvae, have stripes running across their bodies rather than lengthwise. The subfamily is small, only five species occurring in Ontario and Quebec.

Androloma mac-cullochi (Kirby)

Fig. 5

This species is distributed from British Columbia to Labrador. It occurs in northern Quebec and northern Ontario, where the southernmost record is from Sudbury. The adult may be collected in June. The larva feeds on fireweed (*Epilobium* spp.).

Alypia octomaculata (Fabricius)

Figs. 1, 2

The eightspotted forester, *A. octomaculata,* is easily mistaken for *Alypia langtoni*, whose description follows. The female, however, has two white spots on the hind wing and the male, although it may have some dark scaling along the inner margin of the hind wing, does not have a definite black submarginal band. The species occurs in eastern and central North America. It is distributed in the southern part of Quebec and Ontario from Montreal to Point Pelee, Ont. The adult is diurnal, and may be collected during June. The larva, which feeds on grape (*Vitis* spp.) and Virginia creeper (*Parthenocissus* spp.), is marked with black, white, and orange transverse lines.

Alypia langtoni Couper

Figs. 3, 4

A. langtoni is very similar to the preceding species, but the female has only one pale yellow spot on the hind wing and the male has a definite black submarginal band along the inner margin. The species is distributed from Alaska to Nova Scotia. In Ontario and Quebec, it is generally of northern distribution but it occurs as far south as the Ottawa region. The adult may be collected during June. The larva feeds on fireweed (*Epilobium* spp.).

Euthisanotia grata (Fabricius)

Fig. 6

The beautiful wood nymph, *E. grata*, is similar to *Euthisanotia unio*, the following species, except it is larger and has a green line on the inside of the dark border of the fore wing. In *E. grata* the green line is even, whereas in *E. unio* it is wavy. The species is distributed from Windsor to Ottawa and southward through Ontario. There are no specimens from Quebec in the CNC. The moth may be collected in June and early July. The larva feeds on grape (*Vitis* spp.) and Virginia creeper (*Parthenocissus* spp.).

Euthisanotia unio Hübner

Fig. 7

The pearly wood nymph, *E. unio*, is similar to *E. grata* but smaller. The moth is distributed from Windsor to Ottawa. The only specimen from Quebec is from Meach Lake, in the western part of the province. The moth may be collected from late June to late July. The larva feeds on fireweed (*Epilobium* spp.), loosestrife (*Lythrum* spp.), and evening-primrose (*Oenothera* spp.).

Subfamily Pantheinae

The Pantheinae is a small subfamily of predominantly gray, nocturnal moths. The larvae, which are densely hairy except in the genus *Raphia*, feed on the foliage of trees.

Colocasia flavicornis (Smith)

Fig. 8

According to records in the CNC, the species is distributed through the central and southern parts of Ontario and Quebec, from the Manitoba border to Shawinigan, Que. The adult may be collected during May and June. The larva has been reared on beech (*Fagus grandifolia* Ehrh.) and ironwood (*Ostrya virginiana* (Mill.) K. Koch). The species is not common.

Colocasia propinquilinea (Grote)

Fig. 9

The species is distributed from southwestern Ontario to the Ottawa Valley and the Eastern Townships of Quebec. The adult may be collected during May, June, and July. The larva feeds on most broad-leaved trees.

Panthea acronyctoides (Walker)

Fig. 10

This species occurs in the central regions of Ontario and Quebec, from Smoky Falls and Biscotasing, Ont., to Mistassini Post and the Gaspé Peninsula, Que., and southward to the Ottawa region. The moth may be collected during June and July. The larva feeds on spruce (*Picea* spp.) and pine (*Pinus* spp.).

Panthea pallescens McDunnough

Fig. 11

The species is distributed through southern and eastern Ontario and northward to Smoky Falls. In Quebec, it occurs from Laniel to Rivière du Loup. The adult may be collected during June and July. The larva feeds on tamarack (*Larix laricina* (Du Roi) K. Koch) and white pine (*Pinus strobus* L.).

Charadra deridens (Guenée)

Fig. 12

This species occurs in Ontario from Kenora to Ottawa and southward throughout southern Ontario. There are no specimens from Quebec in the CNC. The moth may be collected in June. The larva feeds on white birch (*Betula papyrifera* Marsh.) and oak (*Quercus* spp.).

Raphia frater Grote

Fig. 19

This species is found from British Columbia to Nova Scotia. It is widespread throughout Ontario and Quebec south of the 50th parallel. The moth may be collected in June and July. The larva feeds on trembling aspen (*Populus tremuloides* Michx.).

Subfamily Acronictinae

The subfamily Acronictinae is largely made up of drably colored nocturnal moths, ranging in size from 63 mm (*Acronicta americana*) to 26 mm (*A. exilis*). The larva is hairy; it feeds on a wide variety of trees.

Acronicta rubricoma Guenée

Fig. 23

This species is distributed throughout the eastern half of the United States. It has been collected only at Point Pelee, the southernmost part of Ontario. There are no specimens from Quebec in the CNC. The moth may be collected in June. The larva feeds on hackberry (*Celtis occidentalis* L.).

Acronicta americana Harris

Fig. 25

The American dagger moth is the largest moth in the subfamily. It is commonly found from Alberta to Nova Scotia. The species is distributed across central and southern Ontario and Quebec. The adult may be collected from late May until the end of July. The larva feeds on Manitoba maple (*Acer negundo* L.).

Acronicta dactylina (Grote)

Fig. 26

The species is distributed across Ontario and Quebec, south of Smoky Falls and Mistassini Post. The moth may be collected from May until July. The larva feeds on alder (*Alnus* spp.), birch (*Betula* spp.), and willow (*Salix* spp.).

Acronicta lepusculina Guenée

Fig. 20

The cottonwood dagger moth is distributed across central Ontario from Hymers to Ottawa. Specimens from Quebec in the CNC are from Mistassini Post and Forestville. The adult may be collected from late May until August. The larva feeds on trembling aspen (*Populus tremuloides* Michx.) and willow (*Salix* spp.).

Acronicta leporina (Linnaeus)

Fig. 22

This species has been collected in central and eastern Ontario, and at Montreal, Lac Mondor, and Forestville, Que. The adult may be collected between late May and mid-July. The larva feeds on poplar (*Populus* spp.), willow (*Salix* spp.), and birch (*Betula* spp.).

Acronicta innotata Guenée

Fig. 21

The species is found throughout Ontario and Quebec south of the 50th parallel. The adult may be collected from May until July. The larva feeds on white birch (*Betula papyrifera* Marsh.) and trembling aspen (*Populus tremuloides* Michx.).

Acronicta radcliffei (Harvey)

Fig. 27

This species occurs from Hymers to Ottawa, Ont., and from Montreal to the Gaspé Peninsula, Que. It is not common. The adult may be collected from late June until late July. The larva feeds on cherry (*Prunus* spp.) and serviceberry (*Amelanchier* spp.).

Acronicta tritona (Hübner)

Fig. 24

The species is represented in the CNC by specimens from the central and southern parts of Ontario and from Quebec. This species is widespread but not common. The adult may be collected in May and June. The larva feeds on blueberry (*Vaccinium* spp.).

Acronicta grisea Walker

Fig. 28

The species is distributed from Alberta to Labrador. It is prevalent in Ontario and Quebec between the 45th and 50th parallels. The adult may be collected from June until August. The larva feeds on willow (*Salix* spp.), white birch (*Betula papyrifera* Marsh.), and alder (*Alnus* spp.).

Acronicta albarufa (Grote)

Fig. 29

This species is represented in the CNC by one specimen from Grand Bend, Ont. The adult occurs in July. The larva feeds on bur oak (*Quercus macrocarpa* Michx.).

Acronicta connecta Grote

Fig. 30

The species is represented in the CNC by two specimens from Ancaster, Ont. This is usually a southern species. The adult may be collected in July. The larva feeds on willow (*Salix* spp.).

Acronicta funeralis Grote & Robinson

Fig. 31

The species is widespread throughout central and southern Ontario and Quebec but is not common. The adult may be collected from May until July. The larva feeds on most deciduous trees, such as hickory (*Carya* spp.), birch (*Betula* spp.), elm (*Ulmus* spp.), apple (*Pyrus* spp.), and maple (*Acer* spp.).

Acronicta quadrata (Grote)

Fig. 32

The specimens in the CNC were collected from northwestern Ontario as far east as Thunder Bay. The adult may be collected in June. The larva feeds on cherry and plum (*Prunus* spp.).

Acronicta vinnula (Grote)

Fig. 33

This species is found throughout southern Ontario, from Chatham to Ottawa, and at Norway Bay, in western Quebec. The adult may be collected from June until early August. The larva feeds on elm (*Ulmus* spp.).

Acronicta superans Guenée

Fig. 34

The species occurs across central and southern Ontario from Hymers to Ottawa and eastward to Mt. Lyall, Que. The adult may be collected from May until August. The larva feeds on apple (*Pyrus* spp.) and white birch (*Betula papyrifera* Marsh.).

Acronicta laetifica Smith

Fig. 35

This rare species is distributed from eastern Ontario eastward to Baie Comeau, Que. The adult occurs in July. The larva feeds on hickory (*Carya* spp.).

Acronicta furcifera Guenée

Fig. 36

This species occurs across Ontario and Quebec from Hymers to Lac Mondor, and southward to Ottawa, and in the Eastern Townships of Quebec. The adult may be collected from late June to early August. The larva feeds on cherry (*Prunus* spp.).

Acronicta hasta Guenée

Fig. 38

This species is easily mistaken for *A. furcifera*. It is represented in the CNC by material from southern and eastern Ontario. There is no material from Quebec in the CNC. The moth may be collected during July. The food plant of the larva is cherry (*Prunus* spp.).

Acronicta spinigera Guenée

Fig. 13

This rare species has been collected in both Quebec and Ontario, but only in the vicinity of Ottawa. The adults were collected in June and July. The adult is easily mistaken for *A. morula*, but the fore wing is more mottled and lacks the yellowish patches present in *A. morula*.

Acronicta morula Grote & Robinson

Fig. 42

This species is represented in the CNC by material from Coldstream, in southern Ontario, to Ottawa and to Meach Lake, in western Quebec. There are two broods: adults may be collected in May and early June, and again in July and August. The larva feeds on most deciduous trees, including elm (*Ulmus* spp.), basswood (*Tilia americana* L.), and cherry (*Prunus* spp.).

Acronicta interrupta Guenée

Fig. 39

This species is distributed from Chatham to Ottawa, Ont., and from Norway Bay, in western Quebec, to Forestville, Que. The adult may be collected from June until August. The larva has been reared on elm (*Ulmus* spp.); it also feeds on apple (*Pyrus* spp.), plum (*Prunus* spp.), and birch (*Betula* spp.).

Acronicta pruni Harris

Fig. 41

This species is represented in the CNC by specimens from southern and eastern Ontario. The adult may be collected in July. The larva feeds on American mountain-ash (*Sorbus americana* Marsh.), apple (*Pyrus* spp.), and cherry and plum (*Prunus* spp.).

Acronicta fragilis (Guenée)

Fig. 40

This species is prevalent throughout Ontario and Quebec from Minaki, in northwestern Ontario, to Forestville, Que. It occurs between the latitudes of Ottawa and Ogoki, Ont. The adult may be collected during June and July. The larva feeds on white birch (*Betula papyrifera* Marsh.), American mountain-ash (*Sorbus americana* Marsh.), and apple (*Pyrus* spp.).

Acronicta ovata Grote

Fig. 43

This species is represented in the CNC by material from southern and eastern Ontario. The adult may be collected in July. The larva feeds on oak (*Quercus* spp.).

Acronicta modica Walker

Fig. 37

This species is represented in the CNC by specimens from southern and eastern Ontario and western Quebec. The adult may be collected in June. The larva feeds on red oak (*Quercus rubra* L.).

Acronicta haesitata (Grote)

Fig. 44

The species is represented in the CNC by material from southern and eastern Ontario. There are no specimens from Quebec in the CNC. The adult may be collected during June and July. White oak (*Quercus alba* L.) is the food plant of the larva. This species is usually distinguishable from *A. modica* by its lack of yellow around the reniform and orbicular spots.

Acronicta clarescens Guenée

Fig. 52

This species is represented in the CNC by specimens from Ottawa and from Meach Lake, in western Quebec. The adult may be collected during June and July. The larva has been found on beech (*Fagus grandifolia* Ehrh.) and pin cherry (*Prunus pensylvanica* L. f.).

Acronicta inclara Smith

Fig. 46

Although this species occurs in Canada from Manitoba to Nova Scotia, the CNC has records from only central and eastern Ontario. The adult occurs in June and July. The larva feeds on white oak (*Quercus alba* L.), chestnut (*Castanea dentata* (Marsh.) Borkh.), and birch (*Betula* spp.).

Acronicta tristis Smith

Fig. 47

This uncommon species has been collected from Grand Bend, Ont. eastward to Montreal, Que. The adult occurs from June until August. The larva feeds on beech (*Fagus grandifolia* Ehrh.) and maple (*Acer* spp.).

Acronicta hamamelis Guenée

Fig. 48

This species is uncommon. The food plant, witchhazel (*Hamamelis virginiana* L.), is common only as far north as southern Ontario, which probably accounts for the single specimen from Ancaster, Ont., in the CNC. The adult occurs in late June.

Acronicta increta Morrison

Fig. 49

This species is similar to *A. inclara*, but the hind wing of *A. increta* is noticeably darker. The CNC has three specimens from Ancaster, Ont. There are no specimens from Quebec in the CNC. The adult may be collected in July; it is not common.

Acronicta retardata (Walker)

Fig. 51

This species is found throughout southern Ontario as far north as Capreol. In Quebec, it has been collected at Norway Bay, Meach Lake, and Knowlton. The adult may be collected from late May until early July. Maple (*Acer* spp.) is the food plant of the larva.

Acronicta subochrea Grote

Fig. 50

The CNC has one specimen of this species from Toronto and one from the vicinity of Hamilton, Ont. There are no specimens from Quebec in the

CNC. This species appears to be rare and little is known about it. The adult occurs from mid-June until mid-July.

Acronicta afficta Grote

Fig. 45

This species is represented in the CNC by two specimens from southern and eastern Ontario. There is no material from Quebec in the CNC. The adult may be collected in June. The larva feeds on oak (*Quercus* spp.).

Acronicta impleta Walker

Fig. 53

The species is prevalent throughout the central and southern regions of Ontario and Quebec. The CNC has specimens from Hymers southward to Simcoe and eastward to Ottawa. In Quebec, it has been collected at Aylmer and Lac Mondor. The adult may be collected in June and July. The larva feeds on elm (*Ulmus* spp.), cherry (*Prunus* spp.), and hickory (*Carya* spp.).

Acronicta sperata Grote

Fig. 54

The CNC has specimens of this species from only eastern Ontario and southwestern Quebec. The adult may be collected from mid-May until late June. Poplar (*Populus* spp.) and alder (*Alnus* spp.) are the food plants of the larva.

Acronicta noctivaga Grote

Fig. 55

This species is prevalent in Ontario south of Hymers and Smoky Falls. It has been collected at Norway Bay and Kazabazua, in western Quebec. The adult may be collected from mid-June until mid-July. The larva feeds on poplar (*Populus* spp.).

Acronicta impressa Walker

Fig. 56

This species is prevalent throughout both Ontario and Quebec south of the 50th parallel. It has been reared on willow (*Salix* spp.) and poplar (*Populus* spp.). The adult may be collected during June and July.

Acronicta lithospila Grote

Fig. 58

This species and the two whose descriptions follow are easily distinguishable from the rest of the subfamily by their wing markings, which are unlike the other species of *Acronicta*. This species is represented in the CNC by specimens from southern and eastern Ontario. The adult may be collected in June and July. The larva feeds on red oak (*Quercus rubra* L.), hickory (*Carya* spp.), and chestnut (*Castanea dentata* (Marsh.) Borkh.).

Acronicta oblinita (J. E. Smith)

Fig. 57

The smeared dagger moth is prevalent throughout both Ontario and Quebec south of the 50th parallel. The adult may be collected during June and July. The larva feeds on smartweed (*Polygonum* spp.).

Acronicta lanceolaria (Grote)

Fig. 61

This species is similar to *A. oblinita* but with somewhat narrower, more sharply angled wings. The pure white hind wing lacks the marginal row of dark spots found in *A. oblinita* and the marginal brown shading found in *A. lithospila*. The CNC has material from central and eastern Ontario. There are no specimens from Quebec in the CNC. The adult occurs in June; it is not common. The larva has been reared on largetooth aspen (*Populus grandidentata* Michx.); it also feeds on willow (*Salix* spp.) and cherry (*Prunus* spp.).

Simyra henrici (Grote)

Fig. 60

This species looks more like a *Leucania* (Hadeninae) than an Acronictinae. It is prevalent in Ontario south of Smoky Falls and in western and southern Quebec. The adult may be collected during July and August. Grasses (Gramineae) and smartweed (*Polygonum* spp.) are the food plants of this species.

Harrisimemna trisignata (Walker)

Fig. 59

Although this species is widespread across central and southern Ontario and Quebec, it is not common. The adult occurs in July. The larva feeds on lilac (*Syringa* spp.), ash (*Fraxinus* spp.), and willow (*Salix* spp.).

Subfamily Noctuinae

The subfamily Noctuinae contains nearly 400 species of dull-colored moths. Most of the cutworms of economic importance belong to this subfamily, including the genus *Euxoa*, the largest in the subfamily. Noctuinae do not have hairs on the surface of their eyes and they lack eyelashes. The mid- and hind tibiae are spined. These characters also apply to the subfamily Heliothidinae, but the heliothids often have elliptoid eyes and many species are diurnal.

Although relatively few species of the genus *Euxoa* occur in Ontario and Quebec, in western North America the genus is the most widespread and economically important of the genera in the Noctuinae on the continent. A moth belonging to the genus *Euxoa* is usually recognizable by the presence of a raised tubercule on the head between the eyes.

Euxoa servita (Smith)

Fig. 63

This species occurs from Sault Ste. Marie, Ont., to Lac Mondor, Que., and southward to Lake Ontario. The moth may be collected from mid-July to mid-August. This species is often mistaken for *Euxoa redimicula*, but the hind wing of *E. servita* is entirely dark.

Euxoa redimicula (Morrison)

Fig. 64

This species is found in the same range as *E. servita* in Quebec and Ontario, and also in southern Ontario. The adult may be collected from mid-August to mid-September. Often only the margin of the hind wing is dark. The date of capture is often useful in distinguishing this species from *E. servita*.

Euxoa obeliscoides (Guenée)

Fig. 68

Although this species may be found throughout Canada, the CNC only has specimens from eastern Ontario and western Quebec. The adult occurs in August. The food plant is not known.

Euxoa albipennis (Grote)

Fig. 65

This species is distributed across southern and eastern Ontario and western Quebec. The moth may be collected in August and September.

Euxoa campestris (Grote)

Fig. 86

This species occurs across the central regions of both Ontario and Quebec from Black Sturgeon Lake, in western Ontario, to the Gaspé Peninsula, Que. It has been collected as far north as Ogoki, Ont., and as far south as Meach Lake, Que. The adult may be collected from late July to late August.

Euxoa declarata (Walker)

Fig. 66

This species has been collected across southern and eastern Ontario and in Quebec as far east as Forestville. The adult may be collected from late August until mid-September.

Euxoa tessellata (Harris)

Fig. 69

This species, the striped cutworm, is widespread throughout both Ontario and Quebec south of the 50th parallel. The adult may be collected in July. The larva is occasionally a pest on tobacco in southern Ontario. The moth has an extremely variable wing pattern but can usually be recognized by the presence of a yellow or white tuft of scales at the base of each fore wing.

Euxoa bostoniensis (Grote)

Fig. 70

This species has been collected in southern and southeastern Ontario. There are no specimens in the CNC from Quebec. The adult may be collected in September.

Euxoa ontario (Smith)

Fig. 71

This uncommon species occurs from Black Sturgeon Lake, Ont., through the central regions of Ontario and Quebec to the Gaspé Peninsula, Que. It occurs as far south as Montreal. The moth occurs during August.

Euxoa fumalis (Grote)

Fig. 72

This is the southern counterpart of *E. ontario*. It is found in southern Ontario as far north as Ottawa and southwestern Quebec. It is larger, redder, and lacks the contrasting shades found in *E. ontario*.

Euxoa scholastica McDunnough

Fig. 73

This uncommon species has been collected in southern and eastern Ontario and in western Quebec. The adult may be collected in July and August.

Euxoa ochrogaster (Guenée)

Figs. 84, 85

This species has been collected from Black Sturgeon Lake, Ont., eastward to the Gaspé Peninsula, Que., and from James Bay to Ottawa and Montreal. The adult may be collected during August and early September. The larva, commonly called the redbacked cutworm, is a serious pest of many forage crops.

Euxoa mimallonis (Grote)

Fig. 75

Specimens have been collected at Black Sturgeon Lake and Biscotasing, Ont., and Lac Mondor and Forestville, Que. The adult may be collected in August.

Euxoa velleripennis (Grote)

Fig. 76

This dark moth is found throughout both Ontario and Quebec south of North Bay. The moth may be collected in August.

Euxoa detersa (Walker)

Fig. 77

This species is found throughout both Ontario and Quebec, usually in sandy areas. It can sometimes develop into a serious infestation, damaging tobacco and garden crops. The adult may be collected in September.

Euxoa quebecensis (Smith)

Fig. 78

This species is prevalent along the 50th parallel from Black Sturgeon Lake, Ont., eastward to Natashquan, Que. The adult may be collected from June until August.

Euxoa scandens (Riley)

Fig. 91

This species, commonly called the white cutworm, is found throughout both Ontario and Quebec from Ft. Frances, Ont., to Ste. Anne de Bellevue, Que. The adult may be collected in July. Sweetclover (*Melilotus* spp.) is one of its chief hosts, but it is found also on a wide variety of herbaceous plants.

Euxoa aurulenta (Smith)

Fig. 80

This species is represented in the CNC by specimens from Port Colborne, Ont. There is no material from Quebec in the CNC. The adult may be collected in early June.

Euxoa churchillensis (McDunnough)

Fig. 81

This subarctic species occurs from Hudson Bay westward. The only specimen in the CNC collected in Ontario is from Cape Henrietta Maria. The adult may be collected in July and early August.

Euxoa chimoensis Hardwick

Fig. 82

This rare moth is known only from two specimens collected in late July at Fort Chimo, Que. but it probably occurs in other locations in northwestern Quebec. The adult may be collected in mid-August.

Euxoa pleuritica (Grote)

Fig. 83

This species occurs from the north shore of Lake Superior southward to Toronto and eastward to Montreal, Que. The moth may be collected from early July to mid-August.

Euxoa dissona (Möschler)

Fig. 62

This subarctic species is represented in the CNC by specimens from Indian House Lake, Knob Lake, and Fort Chimo, in northern Quebec. The adult may be collected during July and August. The food plant is not known.

Euxoa perpolita (Morrison)

Fig. 90

This species has been collected in Ontario as far north as Smoky Falls, and in Quebec from Norway Bay to Forestville. The moth may be collected in August.

Euxoa ridingsiana (Grote)

Fig. 16

Geraldton, Ont., is the only location in Ontario or Quebec where this western species has been collected.

Euxoa manitobana McDunnough

Fig. 79

The only record from Ontario or Quebec in the CNC is from Grand Bend, Ont., which is the easternmost record for this species. The moth occurs in July.

Euxoa messoria (Harris)

Fig. 74

This species is prevalent throughout Ontario and Quebec. The darksided cutworm is an important pest of tobacco in southern Ontario and is often common in gardens. The adult may be collected in September.

Euxoa sinelinea Hardwick

Fig. 17

This species occurs in the central region of Ontario and Quebec from Black Sturgeon Lake, Ont., to Montmorency County, Que. It has been collected as far south as Sudbury, Ont. The adult may be collected during July.

Euxoa divergens (Walker)

Fig. 67

This species occurs throughout Ontario and Quebec from Black Sturgeon Lake, Ont., to Lac Mondor, Que., and southward to Knowlton and Ottawa. The adult may be collected in June and July. The food plant is not known.

Euxoa drewseni (Staudinger)

Fig. 18

This uncommon species is represented in the CNC by specimens from Ottawa and from Fort Chimo, Que. The moth occurs from mid-July until mid-August.

Agrotis vetusta Walker

Fig. 92

This species is distributed from Nova Scotia to British Columbia. It is prevalent throughout Ontario and Quebec, from the Manitoba border eastward to Forestville, Que. The moth may be collected during August and September. The food plant is not known.

Agrotis mollis Walker

Fig. 93

This species is represented in the CNC by specimens from Norway Bay, Mistassini Post, and Lac Mondor, Que., and western and central Ontario. The adult may be collected during July and August.

Agrotis patula Walker

Fig. 94

This species is widespread across the subarctic regions of Canada. The CNC has specimens from Knob Lake and Great Whale River, Que. There is no material from Ontario in the CNC. The adult may be collected in July.

Agrotis gladiaria Morrison

Fig. 95

The moth flies mostly in the daytime. Specimens have been collected in southern and eastern Ontario and also near Montreal. The adult may be collected in September. The larva feeds on grasses (Gramineae).

Agrotis venerabilis Walker

Fig. 96

This species is common throughout Canada. It is widespread in Ontario and Quebec. The adult may be collected in September. The larva feeds on white clover (*Trifolium repens* L.).

Agrotis volubilis Harvey

Fig. 97

This species occurs in southern Ontario and Quebec, from Port Colborne to Lac Mondor. The adult may be collected in late May and June.

Agrotis obliqua (Smith)

Fig. 98

This western species is represented in the CNC by specimens from as far east as Larder Lake, Sudbury, and St. Thomas, Ont. The moth may be collected in June.

Agrotis ipsilon (Hufnagel)

Fig. 99

This species is widespread in Ontario and Quebec. The larva, commonly called the black cutworm, feeds on almost any field or garden plant, especially seedlings. The moth may be collected from July until September.

Feltia jaculifera (Guenée)

Fig. 100

This species is represented in the CNC by specimens from the southern parts of Ontario and Quebec, from Windsor to Lac Mondor. The larva feeds on tobacco and garden crops. The adult may be collected in August.

Feltia subgothica (Haworth)

Fig. 103

This species, commonly called the dingy cutworm, occurs across the southern parts of Ontario and Quebec, from Simcoe to Lac Mondor. It is common in tobacco fields, but is not considered a pest. The adult may be collected in July and August.

Feltia herilis (Grote)

Fig. 102

This species is common across the southern parts of Ontario and Quebec, from Teeswater, Ont., to Forestville, Que. The moth may be collected in July and August.

Feltia geniculata (Grote & Robinson)

Fig. 101

Although this species is considered uncommon, it has been collected throughout the southern parts of Ontario and Quebec and as far east as Lac Mondor, Que. The adult may be collected in August and September.

Actebia fennica (Tauscher)

Fig. 104

The CNC has representatives of this species collected from Ottawa northward to the 50th parallel of both Ontario and Quebec. The moth may be collected from July until September. The larva, commonly called the black army cutworm, damages blueberry (*Vaccinium* spp.) and some forage crops.

Spaelotis clandestina (Harris)

Fig. 105

This species is common throughout both Ontario and Quebec as far north as James Bay. The adult may be collected from July until September. The larva, called the w-marked cutworm, feeds on blueberry (*Vaccinium* spp.).

Choephora fungorum Grote & Robinson

Fig. 106

The CNC has only two specimens of this species from Ontario, one from Chatham and the other from Port Colborne. The moth may be collected in September. The larva feeds on dandelion (*Taraxacum* spp.).

Eurois occulta (Linnaeus)

Fig. 111

The adult of this species is the largest in the subfamily. It is widely distributed throughout Canada and is prevalent in Ontario and Quebec. The moth may be collected in July and August. Tamarack (*Larix laricina* (Du Roi) K. Koch) is the food plant of the larva.

Eurois astricta Morrison

Fig. 108

This species is present in both Ontario and Quebec as far north as the 50th parallel. The adult may be collected in July and August. The larva feeds on trembling aspen (*Populus tremuloides* Michx.).

Ochropleura plecta (Linnaeus)

Fig. 107

This species is common in Ontario and Quebec as far north as James Bay. The adult may be collected from May until August. The larva feeds on clover (*Trifolium* spp.).

Euagrotis illapsa (Walker)

Fig. 112

This species is represented in the CNC by material from southern and eastern Ontario. There are no specimens from Quebec in the CNC. The adult may be collected in June and again in August.

Euagrotis forbesi Franclemont

Fig. 116

This species is very similar to *E. illapsa*, but is somewhat larger. The CNC has specimens from southern and eastern Ontario and from Montreal, Qué. The adult may be collected in July and August.

Metalepsis fishii (Grote)

Fig. 115

The CNC has specimens of this uncommon species that were collected from western Ontario to western Quebec. The moth occurs in May. The larva feeds on blueberry (*Vaccinium* spp.).

Metalepsis salicarum (Walker)

Fig. 109

The species occurs across both Ontario and Quebec, from Hymers, in northwestern Ontario, to the Gaspé Peninsula, Que. The moth may be collected in late April and May.

Cerastis tenebrifera (Walker)

Fig. 110

This species is represented in the CNC by specimens from southern and eastern Ontario and from Kirk's Ferry to Lac Mondor, Que. The adult may be collected in May. The larva feeds on dandelion (*Taraxacum* spp.).

Peridroma saucia (Hübner)

Fig. 114

This moth is prevalent throughout both Ontario and Quebec. The larva, commonly called the variegated cutworm, has many hosts, such as field and garden crops and flowers. The adult may be collected from May until September.

Hemipachnobia monochromatea (Morrison)

Fig. 113

This species is represented by specimens from the Mer Bleue, Ont., and Mistassini Post, Que. The food plants, sundew (*Drosera* spp.) and cranberry (*Vaccinium* spp.), grow in peat bogs. The restricted nature of the habitat may account for its apparent scarcity. The moth may be collected in June.

Paradiarsia littoralis (Packard)

Fig. 117

This species occurs across both Ontario and Quebec, from Smoky Falls, Ont., to Bradore Bay, Que., and from Ottawa northward to James Bay. The adult may be collected in June and July. The larva feeds on dandelion (*Taraxacum* spp.), plantain (*Plantago* spp.), and clover (*Trifolium* spp.).

Graphiphora haruspica (Grote)

Fig. 118

This species is widespread throughout Ontario and Quebec. The larva feeds on willow (*Salix* spp.). The adult may be collected in July and August.

Rhyacia quadrangula (Zetterstedt)

Fig. 121

This species is represented in the CNC by material from the subarctic region of Quebec. The adult may be collected in July.

Chersotis juncta (Grote)

Fig. 14

The CNC has only one specimen of this primarily western species that was collected from Ontario or Quebec. It was collected at Meach Lake, Que. The moth occurs during July. The larva feeds on clover (*Trifolium* spp.), sweetclover (*Melilotus* spp.), and campion (*Lychnis* spp.).

Heptagrotis phyllophora (Grote)

Fig. 120

This species occurs across the central regions of both Ontario and Quebec, from Ogoki, Ont., to Natashquan, on the north shore of the Gulf of St. Lawrence, and southward to the Mer Bleue, Ont. The moth may be collected in late June and July. The food plants of the larvae are cherry (*Prunus* spp.), alder (*Alnus* spp.), birch (*Betula* spp.), blueberry (*Vaccinium* spp.), arrowwood (*Viburnum* spp.), and willow (*Salix* spp.).

Diarsia rubifera (Grote)

Fig. 119

This species occurs across the central regions of both Ontario and Quebec, from Hymers, Ont., to Lac Mondor, Que., and southward to Ottawa. The moth may be collected in July and August.

Diarsia dislocata (Smith)

Fig. 122

This species is represented in the CNC by specimens from Schefferville, Lac Mondor, and Mt. Lyall, Que. There is no material from Ontario in the CNC. The adult may be collected in August.

Diarsia jucunda (Walker)

Fig. 123

This species occurs from Hymers, Ont., eastward across the central regions of Ontario and Quebec to Lac Mondor, Que. The moth may be collected in July. The larva feeds on grasses (Gramineae).

Diarsia pseudorosaria freemani Hardwick

Fig. 15

This northern and western species has been collected in Ontario at Hymers and Ogoki, and in Quebec at Mistassini Post and near Kamouraska. The adult may be collected from mid-July until mid-August.

Amathes c-nigrum (Linnaeus)

Fig. 124

This species, commonly called the spotted cutworm, is found throughout both Ontario and Quebec as far north as James Bay. The first brood flies in May, and the second in September. Goosefoot (*Chenopodium* spp.) is the food plant of the larva.

Amathes smithii (Snellen)

Fig. 125

The species in common throughout both Ontario and Quebec. The adult may be collected during July and August.

Amathes badinodis (Grote)

Fig. 126

The CNC has specimens from southern and eastern Ontario and western Quebec. The adult may be collected in September. The larva feeds on dock (*Rumex* spp.) and chickweed (*Stellaria* spp.).

Amathes normaniana (Grote)

Fig. 127

This species occurs commonly throughout Ontario and Quebec during August. The larva feeds on plantain (*Plantago* spp.).

A similar species, *Amathes oblata* (Morrison), with an orange-red fore wing and an orange border, has recently been collected in western Ontario and northern Quebec in July.

Amathes xanthographa (Fabricius)

Fig. 88

The European species has become established in several parts of North America. The only collections from Ontario or Quebec are two specimens captured in Montreal in mid-July. The larva feeds on dock (*Rumex* spp.) and plantain (*Plantago* spp.).

Amathes collaris (Grote & Robinson)

Fig. 128

The CNC has material from central and southern Ontario and Quebec. The moth may be collected during August and September.

Amathes bicarnea (Guenée)

Fig. 129

The CNC has specimens from southern and eastern Ontario northward to Lake Nipissing, and from Meach Lake, in western Quebec, eastward to Lac Mondor. The moth may be collected in July and August. The larva feeds on blueberry (*Vaccinium* spp.), gray birch (*Betula populifolia* Marsh.), dandelion (*Taraxacum* spp.), maple (*Acer* spp.), and meadowsweet (*Spiraea alba* Du Roi).

Amathes tenuicula (Morrison)

Fig. 130

Although this species is uncommon, it is widespread across both Ontario and Quebec from James Bay southward. The moth may be collected during July and August.

Amathes opacifrons (Grote)

Fig. 131

This species is common in bogs, where its food plant, blueberry (*Vaccinium* spp.), occurs. The CNC has material from Ogoki and Mer Bleue, Ont., and from Mistassini Post and Trinity Bay, Que. The adult may be collected from late June until August.

Pachnobia tecta (Hübner)

Fig. 132

The CNC has material of this subarctic species from Knob Lake northward to Fort Chimo, Que. There are no specimens from Ontario in the CNC. The moth occurs in July and early August.

Pachnobia wockei (Möschler)

Fig. 87

This species has been collected at Knob Lake, Que., in late July and early August. There are no specimens from Ontario in the CNC.

Pachnobia scropulana (Morrison)

Fig. 133

The CNC has material of this species from Knob Lake and Indian House Lake, in northern Quebec. The adult may be collected in July.

Pachnobia okakensis (Packard)

Fig. 134

This species is found at Knob Lake and Indian House Lake, in northern Quebec. The moth may be collected in July.

Anomogyna atrata (Morrison)

Fig. 135

This species is found across both Ontario and Quebec, from Black Sturgeon Lake, Ont., northward to Knob Lake, Que. The moth may be collected during July and August.

Anomogyna fabulosa Ferguson

Fig. 136

This uncommon species is represented in the CNC by material from Montmorency, Que. The adult occurs in July.

Anomogyna speciosa (Hübner)

Fig. 137

The CNC has only one specimen, from Lac Jacques Cartier in Laurentide Park, Qué. The more northerly subspecies, *A. speciosa mixta* Wlk., is found in northern Quebec at Knob Lake and Indian House Lake. Both subspecies may be collected during July.

Anomogyna perquiritata (Morrison)

Fig. 138

The CNC has only one specimen from Ontario, from Black Sturgeon Lake. In Quebec, it has been collected from the Gaspé Peninsula and Mistassini Post northward to Fort Chimo. The adult may be collected during July and August. The larva feeds on black spruce (*Picea mariana* (Mill.) B.S.P.) and white spruce (*Picea glauca* (Moench) Voss).

Anomogyna laetabilis (Zetterstedt)

Fig. 89

This subarctic species is represented in the CNC by one specimen from Indian House Lake, in northern Quebec. The adult occurs in July and early August.

Anomogyna homogena McDunnough

Fig. 139

The CNC has material of this species from the Gaspé Peninsula northward to Fort Chimo, Que. The moth may be collected in August.

Anomogyna imperita (Hübner)

Fig. 140

This species is prevalent across northern Quebec from Port Harrison eastward to Indian House Lake and southward to Mistassini Post. The moth may be collected from mid-July until mid-August.

Anomogyna elimata (Guenée)

Fig. 141

This species is found across both Ontario and Quebec south of James Bay. The larva feeds on white spruce (*Picea glauca* (Moench) Voss) and jack pine (*Pinus banksiana* Lamb.). The adult may be collected during July and August.

Anomogyna dilucida (Morrison)

Fig. 142

The CNC has material from eastern Ontario and from Laniel and Meach Lake, in western Quebec, to Forestville. The larva feeds on tamarack (*Larix laricina* (Du Roi) K. Koch) and black spruce (*Picea mariana* (Mill.) B.S.P.). The adult may be collected in August and early September.

Anomogyna youngii (Smith)

Fig. 143

This species is commonly found in acid bogs, where the larva feeds on blueberry (*Vaccinium* spp.). The specimens in the CNC are from eastern Ontario. There is no material from Quebec in the CNC. The moth may be collected during August and September.

Aplectoides condita (Guenée)

Fig. 144

This species is not common; it is distributed across western and central Ontario to western Quebec. The moth occurs in June and July.

Anaplectoides pressus (Grote)

Fig. 145

This species is present throughout both Ontario and Quebec from Ogoki to Forestville and southward. The moth may be collected from June until August.

Anaplectoides prasina (Schiffermüller)

Fig. 149

The CNC has material of this species from Ogoki, Ont., eastward to Forestville and the Gaspé Peninsula, Que., and southward to Toronto and Meach Lake, near Ottawa. The adult may be collected in July and August.

Protolampra rufipectus (Morrison)

Fig. 147

This species occurs across the central regions of both Ontario and Quebec from Hymers, in northwestern Ontario, eastward to Forestville, Que., and southward to Ottawa. The moth may be collected in August.

Protolampra brunneicollis (Grote)

Fig. 148

This species has been collected in southern and eastern Ontario as well as western Quebec. The larva feeds on dandelion (*Taraxacum* spp.) and sweet-fern (*Comptonia peregrina* (L.) Coult.). The adult may be collected in July.

Cryptocala acadiensis (Bethune)

Fig. 146

This species is widespread across Canada and is prevalent in central and northern Ontario and Quebec as far north as James Bay. The moth may be collected during July and August.

Eueretagrotis sigmoides (Guenée)

Fig. 150

The CNC has specimens of this species from Trenton, Ont., eastward to Lac Mondor, Que. The moth may be collected in July and early August.

Eueretagrotis perattenta (Grote)

Figs. 151, 153

This species is prevalent across Ontario and Quebec as far north as James Bay. The moth may be collected in July.

Eueretagrotis attenta (Grote)

Fig. 152

This species occurs across the central regions of Ontario and Quebec from Hymers, in northwestern Ontario, eastward to Lac Mondor and St. Pascal, at the foot of the Gaspé Peninsula, Que. The adult may be collected in July.

Abagrotis alternata (Grote)

Fig. 154

This species is found from southern and eastern Ontario eastward to Lac Mondor, Que. The moth may be collected in August.

Rhynchagrotis cupida (Grote)

Fig. 161

This species occurs across southern and eastern Ontario northward to Sudbury, and in Quebec from Kazabazua to Forestville. The moth may be collected from July until September.

Rhynchagrotis anchocelioides (Guenée)

Fig. 156

This uncommon species is represented in the CNC by specimens from the Niagara Peninsula, Ottawa, Montreal, and Meach Lake, in western Quebec. The adult occurs from late July until early August.

Ufeus satyricus Grote

Fig. 157

This species is found from Hymers to Ottawa, Ont., and Lac Mondor, Que. The adult may be collected in September and October.

Subfamily Hadeninae

The subfamily Hadeninae includes about 50 genera and 480 species in Canada and the United States. Hadeninae caterpillars are often called armyworms, but this common name is also used for other noctuids. Some of the more important pests in this subfamily are the armyworm (*Pseudaletia unipuncta* (Haworth)), the wheat head armyworm (*Faronta diffusa* (Walker)), and the bronzed cutworm (*Nephelodes minians* Guenée). The adults of the subfamily Hadeninae are easily recognizable by the hair on the surface of their eyes.

Scotogramma trifolii (Rottenburg)

Fig. 158

This species is widespread throughout the temperate areas of Canada. The CNC has specimens from central and southern Ontario and Quebec. It is considered a minor pest of clover (*Trifolium* spp.) and is commonly called the clover cutworm. The adult may be collected from June until August.

Tricholea artesta (Smith)

Fig. 159

The CNC has material of this species from the Chatham and Port Colborne regions of southern Ontario. There are no specimens from Quebec in the CNC. The adult may be collected in October; this species may be a migrant.

Mamestra curialis (Smith)

Fig. 160

This species is found from Hymers, in western Ontario, to Forestville, Que. The moth may be collected in July. The larva feeds on clover (*Trifolium* spp.), grasses (Gramineae), and dandelion (*Taraxacum* spp.).

Polia nimbosa (Guenée)

Fig. 155

This species occurs across the central regions of Ontario and Quebec from Black Sturgeon Lake eastward to Lac Mondor. The food plants of the larva are huckleberry (*Gaylussacia* spp.) and maple (*Acer* spp.). The moth may be collected in July.

Polia leomegra (Smith)

Fig. 171

Little is known about this species. The CNC has only one specimen from Black Sturgeon Lake, Ont. The moth occurs in July.

Polia carbonifera (Hampson)

Fig. 166

Although primarily of western distribution, this species occurs in the east across central Ontario and Quebec to Labrador. The CNC has specimens from Ogoki, Ont., and Lac Mondor and Knob Lake, Que. The adult may be collected from mid-July to early August.

Polia imbrifera (Guenée)

Fig. 174

This species is prevalent from Hymers, Ont., eastward to Rivière du Loup, Que., and from James Bay southward to Ottawa. The adult may be collected in July and August. Red choke cherry (*Prunus virginiana* L.) is the host plant of the larva.

Polia purpurissata (Grote)

Fig. 177

This species is widespread throughout Ontario and Quebec as far north as James Bay. The moth may be collected in July and August. The larva feeds on willow (*Salix* spp.).

Polia grandis (Boisduval)

Fig. 175

This species is prevalent across Ontario and Quebec as far north as Black Sturgeon Lake and Forestville. The adult may be collected from June until August. The larva feeds on willow (*Salix* spp.) and cherry (*Prunus* spp.).

Polia subjuncta (Grote & Robinson)

Fig. 176

This species is represented in the CNC by material from southern and eastern Ontario and Kazabazua, in western Quebec. The larva feeds on willow (*Salix* spp.), alder (*Alnus* spp.), maple (*Acer* spp.), and poplar (*Populus* spp.). There are two broods; the moth may be collected in May and June, and again in July and August.

Polia latex (Guenée)

Fig. 178

This species is found from southern and eastern Ontario to Lac Mondor, Que. The adult may be collected in June. The larva feeds on yellow birch (*Betula alleghaniensis* Britton).

Polia atlantica (Grote)

Fig. 173

This species occurs from Smoky Falls, Ont., southward to Ottawa and Knowlton, Que. The larval hosts are clover (*Trifolium* spp.), plantain (*Plantago* spp.), and dandelion (*Taraxacum* spp.). The moth may be collected in June and July.

Polia nevadae (Grote)

Fig. 179

The CNC has specimens of this species from Hymers, in northwestern Ontario, eastward to Forestville, Que., and southward to Ottawa. The larva feeds on birch (*Betula* spp.), particularly gray birch (*Betula populifolia* Marsh.). The moth may be collected from mid-June until mid-July.

Polia radix (Walker)

Fig. 180

This species is found across the central regions of Ontario and Quebec from Lake Nipigon eastward to Mistassini Post and southward to Ottawa. The adult may be collected in June. The larva feeds on dandelion (*Taraxacum* spp.), plantain (*Plantago* spp.), and grasses (Gramineae).

Polia segregata (Smith)

Fig. 162

This western species has been collected in both Quebec and Ontario, but only in the vicinity of Ottawa. The early flight period of the adult, late April to mid-May, may account for the lack of records. The larva feeds on plants in the Oleaster family (Elaeagnaceae).

Polia legitima (Grote)

Fig. 181

This species is distributed throughout Ontario and Quebec as far north as the 50th parallel. The larva, commonly called the striped garden caterpillar, feeds on willow (*Salix* spp.). The adult flies from June until August.

Polia tacoma (Strecker)

Fig. 182

This species is found across Ontario from Hymers to Larder Lake, and in Quebec from Hull to Mt. Albert in the Gaspé Peninsula. The adult may be mistaken for *P. legitima*, but *P. tacoma* has more brown on the fore wings and a pale streak extending out of the orbicular spot toward the wing margin. The adult may be collected in June and July. The larva feeds on cherry (*Prunus* spp.) and birch (*Betula* spp.).

Polia rugosa (Morrison)

Fig. 183

This species is found in acid bogs. It is represented in the CNC by material from the Mer Bleue, Ont., and from Laniel and Mistassini Post, Que. The moth may be collected from June until August. The adult can be distinguished from *P. tacoma* by the pale shading on the veins of the fore wing. The larva feeds on black chokeberry (*Aronia melanocarpa* (Michx.) Ell.).

Polia lilacina (Harvey)

Fig. 184

This species is widespread from the Atlantic Provinces to Alberta. The CNC has specimens from as far north as Larder Lake, Ont., and from the Eastern Townships of Quebec. Aster (*Aster* spp.) is the host. The adult may be collected in June.

Polia adjuncta (Boisduval)

Fig. 185

This species is found in the southern regions of both Ontario and Quebec and as far north as Black Sturgeon Lake, Ont., and Lac Mondor and Forestville, Que. The adult may be collected from late May until July and again in August. Larval host plants include elm (*Ulmus americana* L.), dandelion (*Taraxacum* spp.), plantain (*Plantago* spp.), and clover (*Trifolium* spp.).

Polia assimilis (Morrison)

Fig. 186

The CNC has material of this species from Black Sturgeon Lake, in northwestern Ontario to the Ottawa Valley and eastward through the Eastern Townships of Quebec. It has been reared from St. John's-wort (*Hypericum perforatum* L.). The moth may be collected in July.

Polia pulverulenta (Smith)

Fig. 187

This species occurs from Minaki, in northwestern Ontario, eastward to Forestville and Mt. Lyall, Que. The moth is similar to *P. assimilis* but is paler with much more white along the border of the fore wing. The larva feeds on willow (*Salix* spp.), aster (*Aster* spp.), and tamarack (*Larix laricina* (Du Roi) K. Koch). The moth may be collected in July and August.

Polia ingravis (Smith)

Fig. 164

The only records of this western species in the CNC from Ontario are from Sudbury and Larder Lake and those from Quebec are from Indian House Lake. The adult may be collected in July and August.

Polia cristifera (Walker)

Fig. 188

This species is prevalent across the central region of both Ontario and Quebec from Sioux Lookout in western Ontario to Forestville, Que. The moth may be collected during June and July.

Polia lutra (Guenée)

Fig. 189

This species is found across Ontario and Quebec south of Smoky Falls, Ont., and Mistassini Post, Que. The larva feeds on white birch (*Betula papyrifera* Marsh.). The adult may be collected in July and early August.

Polia secedens (Walker)

Fig. 165

This species has been found in Ontario at Black Sturgeon Lake and in Quebec at Mt. Lyall in the Gaspé Peninsula, Knob Lake, and Indian House Lake. The moth may be collected from late June to early August.

Polia detracta (Walker)

Fig. 190

This species is found across both Ontario and Quebec as far north as James Bay. The moth may be collected in July. The larval hosts are the buds of oak (*Quercus* spp.), blueberry (*Vaccinium* spp.), and serviceberry (*Amelanchier* spp.).

Polia goodelli (Grote)

Fig. 191

This species is found in the southern part of both Ontario and Quebec from

Strathroy, Ont., to the Eastern Townships of Quebec, and northward to Sudbury, Ont. The moth may be collected in July.

Polia obscura (Smith)

Fig. 192

This species is found across the central part of Ontario southward to Trenton and eastward to Meach Lake, in western Quebec. The adult may be collected in June.

Lacinipolia meditata (Grote)

Fig. 193

This species occurs across southern and eastern Ontario from Normandale to Ottawa and in Quebec at Lac Mondor. The moth may be collected in August. Dandelion (*Taraxacum officinale* Weber) is the host plant.

Lacinipolia lustralis (Grote)

Fig. 194

This species occurs across central and southern Ontario and Quebec from Hymers eastward to Ottawa and from Norway Bay to Lac Mondor. This species appears to be rare in the southern parts of Ontario and Quebec. The adult may be collected from late June until mid-July. The larva feeds on dandelion (*Taraxacum officinale* Weber) and alfalfa (*Medicago sativa* L.).

Lacinipolia anguina (Grote)

Fig. 195

This species is found in Ontario from Hymers to Smoky Falls and southward to Grand Bend. It has also been collected at Norway Bay, in western Quebec. The moth may be collected in June.

Lacinipolia vicina (Grote)

Fig. 196

The CNC has material of this species from Hymers and Trenton, Ont., and from Meach Lake, in western Quebec. The adult may be collected in July.

Lacinipolia renigera (Stephens)

Fig. 197

This is one of the more common species belonging to this genus. It is found throughout the central and southern parts of Ontario and Quebec. The adult may be collected from late May until early September. The larva, commonly called the bristly cutworm, has been reared on dandelion (*Taraxacum* spp.) and plantain (*Plantago* spp.).

Lacinipolia lorea (Guenée)

Fig. 198

This species occurs throughout both Ontario and Quebec as far north as the 50th parallel. The adult may be collected from late June until mid-July. The larva has been reared on dandelion (*Taraxacum officinale* Weber).

Lacinipolia olivacea (Morrison)

Fig. 199

This species occurs in Ontario and Quebec as far north as the 50th parallel. The moth may be collected in August. The larva feeds on dandelion (*Taraxacum officinale* Weber).

Lacinipolia implicata McDunnough

Fig. 163

This southern species has been reported in Canada only at Chaffey's Locks, north of Kingston, Ont. The adult may be collected in August and September.

Lasionycta albinuda (Smith)

Fig. 167

This rare species is only known from northeastern Canada. It has been collected at Black Sturgeon Lake, Ont. In Quebec, it is found from Granby eastward along the north shore of the St. Lawrence and northward into Labrador. The adult occurs from late June to early August.

Lasionycta subdita (Möschler)

Fig. 200

This subarctic species is represented in the CNC by material from Knob Lake and Indian House Lake in Quebec. No specimens have been collected in Ontario. The adult occurs in July.

Lasiestra phoca (Möschler)

Fig. 201

The CNC has material of this species from Knob Lake and Fort Chimo, in the subarctic region of Quebec. The adult may be collected in July.

Lasiestra uniformis (Smith)

Fig. 202

The CNC has only one specimen of this species; it was collected at Mt. Albert, Que. No material has been collected in Ontario. This species is more common in the west. The adult occurs in July.

Anarta cordigera (Thunberg)

Fig. 203

This species is found in the subarctic region of Quebec at Fort Chimo and Thunder River. In the southern part of Ontario, it has been collected only in the Mer Bleue bog near Ottawa, but it probably occurs in other bogs in Quebec and Ontario. The moth may be collected from mid-May until mid-June. The larva feeds on blueberry (*Vaccinium* spp.) and bearberry (*Arctostaphylos* spp.).

Anarta melanopa (Thunberg)

Fig. 204

This species has been collected from the north shore of the Gulf of St. Lawrence northward in Quebec and at Fort Severn in northernmost Ontario. The adult may be collected in mid-July. The larva feeds on blueberry (*Vaccinium* spp.).

Anarta richardsoni (Curtis)

Fig. 205

This species is found in the arctic region of Quebec at Great Whale River and Payne Bay. No material has been collected from Ontario. The adult may be collected in July.

Sideridis rosea (Harvey)

Fig. 206

This species is common across Ontario and Quebec from Strathroy northward to Sudbury and eastward to Lac Mondor. The adult may be collected in May and June. The host plants are gooseberry (*Ribes* spp.), willow (*Salix* spp.), soapberry (*Sheperdia* spp.), and Russian olive (*Elaeagnus angustifolia* L.).

Sideridis congermana (Morrison)

Fig. 207

The CNC has two specimens, one from Grand Bend, in southern Ontario, and the other from Norway Bay, in western Quebec. This is considered a rare species. The moth occurs in July.

Sideridis maryx (Guenée)

Fig. 208

This species is represented in the CNC by material from Smoky Falls, Ont., and from Forestville, Que. The adult may be collected in June and July. It is not considered a common species.

Astrapetis sutrina (Grote)

Fig. 168

The CNC has one specimen of this species from Bonaventure Island, at the tip of the Gaspé Peninsula of Quebec. The adult may be collected in early July.

Anepia capsularis (Guenée)

Fig. 209

This species has been collected in Ontario as far east as Belleville. It is more common in the south. The adult may be collected in June and is apparently rare. The larva feeds on the capsules of species in the pink family (Caryophyllaceae).

Tricholita signata (Walker)

Fig. 210

This species has been collected in southern and eastern Ontario, and in Quebec from Norway Bay eastward to Lac Mondor. The moth may be collected from July until September.

Ulolonche modesta (Morrison)

Fig. 211

The CNC has material of this species from eastern and southern Ontario. The adult occurs in early June, but does not appear to be common north of the Great Lakes.

Ulolonche culea (Guenée)

Fig. 212

The CNC has representatives of this species from Trenton, Ont., eastward to Lac Mondor, Que. The moth may be collected in June. This species is not considered to be common. The larva has been reared on red oak (*Quercus rubra* L.).

Protorthodes oviduca (Guenée)

Fig. 213

This species is found throughout both Ontario and Quebec as far north as the 50th parallel. The adult may be collected from late May until July. The larva feeds on dandelion (*Taraxacum* spp.), plantain (*Plantago* spp.), and grasses (Gramineae).

Homorthodes furfurata (Grote)

Fig. 214

This species has been collected across Ontario from Hymers to Ottawa, and from southern Quebec as far north as Lac Mondor. The adult may be collected in July. The larva feeds on maple (*Acer* spp.).

Pseudorthodes vecors (Guenée)

Fig. 215

This species is common in both Ontario and Quebec from Hymers and Smoky Falls to Knowlton, in the Eastern Townships of Quebec. The larva feeds on dandelion (*Taraxacum* spp.), plantain (*Plantago* spp.), and grasses (Gramineae). The moth may be collected in July.

Orthodes crenulata (Butler)

Fig. 216

This species occurs in southern and eastern Ontario from Strathroy to Ottawa and in Quebec from Meach Lake to Lac Mondor. The larva has been reared on grasses (Gramineae), dandelion (*Taraxacum* spp.), and plantain (*Plantago* spp.). The moth may be collected in late June and July.

Orthodes cynica Guenée

Fig. 217

This species is common across both Ontario and Quebec as far north as the 50th parallel. The larva has been reared on plantain (*Plantago* spp.). The moth may be collected in late May and June.

Anhimella contrahens (Walker)

Fig. 218

The CNC has material of this species from Hymers, Trenton, Ottawa, and the Muskoka district, in Ontario, and from Meach Lake, in western Quebec. The host plant is dandelion (*Taraxacum officinale* Weber). The moth may be collected during July.

Nephelodes minians Guenée

Fig. 219

This species is prevalent across Ontario and Quebec as far north as James Bay. The larva, commonly called the bronzed cutworm, may cause considerable damage to cereal crops during an infestation. The adult may be collected in August and September.

Morrisonia distincta (Hübner)

Fig. 172

The CNC has specimens of this species from southern and eastern Ontario and Montreal, Que. The larva feeds on maple (*Acer* spp.) and grape (*Vitis* spp.). The adult may be collected in late April and May.

Morrisonia evicta (Grote)

Fig. 220

The CNC has specimens of this species from southern and eastern Ontario, and from Newaygo, in the Laurentian district of Quebec. The larva has been reared on cherry (*Prunus* spp.). The moth may be collected in May.

Morrisonia confusa (Hübner)

Fig. 221

The CNC has material of this species from London eastward to Algonquin Park and Ottawa in Ontario and from Meach Lake eastward to Lac Mondor in Quebec. The larva feeds on basswood (*Tilia americana* L.), poplar (*Populus* spp.), and cherry (*Prunus* spp.). The adult may be collected in May and June.

Xylomyges dolosa Grote

Fig. 222

This species is found in Ontario from Hymers eastward to Ottawa and in Quebec from Kirk's Ferry eastward to Lac Mondor. The adult may be collected in May. The larva feeds on Lombardy poplar (*Populus nigra* var.

italica Muenchh.) and trembling aspen (*Populus tremuloides* Michx.).

Stretchia plusiaeformis Edwards

Fig. 169

This moth has been collected at Black Sturgeon Lake and Smoky Falls, Ont. The adult may be collected in May. The larva feeds on currant (*Ribes* spp.).

Orthosia rubescens (Walker)

Fig. 223

The CNC has material of this species from eastern Ontario and from Lac Mondor, Que. The moth may be collected in late April and May. The larva feeds on maple (*Acer* spp.) and cherry (*Prunus* spp.).

Orthosia revicta (Morrison)

Fig. 224

This species has been found across central and southern Ontario and Quebec from Hymers, Ont., eastward to Lac Mondor, Que. The larva feeds on cherry (*Prunus* spp.), birch (*Betula* spp.), and poplar (*Populus* spp.). The adult may be collected in May.

Orthosia hibisci (Guenée)

Fig. 225

This species is found across Ontario and Quebec as far north as North Bay. The moths are often abundant and may be collected in early May. The larva has been reared on cherry (*Prunus* spp.).

Crocigrapha normani (Grote)

Fig. 226

This species is common across southern and eastern Ontario, and also from Harrington Lake, in western Quebec, eastward to Lac Mondor. The larva feeds on most deciduous trees. The moth may be collected in May and early June.

Ceramica picta (Harris)

Fig. 227

The CNC has material from southern and eastern Ontario and from Beechgrove, in western Quebec. The larva, commonly called the zebra caterpillar, has been reared on dandelion (*Taraxacum officinale* Weber); it also feeds on the foliage of several crop plants. The adult may be collected from June until August.

Faronta diffusa (Walker)

Fig. 228

This species is common across Ontario and Quebec as far north as the 50th parallel. It is one of the more important pests of the subfamily. The larva, commonly called the wheat head armyworm, can cause heavy damage to grasslands and cereal crops. The moth may be collected from May until August.

Leucania linita Guenée

Fig. 170

The CNC has one specimen of this species from Alcove, in western Quebec. The moth may be collected in July.

Leucania pseudargyria Guenée

Fig. 229

This species is found throughout southern Ontario and Quebec, from Simcoe eastward to Lac Mondor. The larva is a pest of cereal grasses such as redtop (*Agrostis alba* L.), timothy (*Phleum pratense* L.), wild rye (*Elymus* spp.), and wheatgrass (*Agropyron* spp.). The moth may be collected during July. The adult may be distinguished from the next two species by the red tint on the fore wing.

Leucania ursula Forbes

Fig. 230

The CNC has material of this species from southern and eastern Ontario, and from Knowlton, in the Eastern Townships of Quebec. The adult may be collected in June and also in September, indicating that there are probably two broods. The larva feeds on honeysuckle (*Lonicera* spp.).

Leucania inermis Forbes

Fig. 231

The CNC has material from southern and eastern Ontario, and from Meach Lake, Knowlton, and Lac Mondor, Que. The larval food plant is orchard grass (*Dactylis glomerata* L.). The moth may be collected in June and July. The male lacks the large tufts of hair present on the front legs of *pseudargyria* and *ursula*.

Leucania commoides Guenée

Fig. 232

This species is fairly common throughout southern Ontario and Quebec from Strathroy, Ont., eastward to Lac Mondor, Que. Orchard grass (*Dactylis glomerata* L.) is the food plant of the larva. The adult may be collected in June and July.

Leucania phragmatidicola Guenée

Fig. 233

This species is found throughout Ontario south of James Bay. There is no material from Quebec in the CNC. Adults may be collected from late May to early October. The larva feeds on grasses (Gramineae).

Leucania multilinea Walker

Fig. 241

This species has been collected across Ontario as far north as Ogoki and in Quebec at Knowlton, in the Eastern Townships. The adult may be collected in June and July. The larva feeds on brome grass (*Bromus* spp.), quack grass (*Agropyron repens* (L.) Beauv.), and orchard grass (*Dactylis glomerata* L.).

Leucania insueta Guenée

Fig. 235

This species is common across Ontario and Quebec as far north as Ogoki and Lac Mondor. The larva feeds on grasses (Gramineae). The moth may be collected in June and July.

Pseudaletia unipuncta (Haworth)

Fig. 236

The larva of this species is commonly called the armyworm. This species is found across both Ontario and Quebec as far north as the 50th parallel. It is a very serious pest of field and garden crops. The moth may be collected from March to November.

Aletia oxygala (Grote)

Fig. 237

This species is found across Ontario and Quebec as far north as the 50th parallel. The moth may be collected from June until September. The larva feeds on grasses (Gramineae).

Subfamily Cuculliinae

The subfamily Cuculliinae has about 70 genera and 325 species in North America. The larvae of this subfamily feed above ground. Many of the species overwinter as an adult that flies in the fall and again in the spring. One identifying character of the Cuculliinae that is not easily detected are the lashes both in front of and behind the eyes of the adults.

Brachionycha borealis (Smith)

Fig. 256

The CNC has specimens of this species from Black Sturgeon Lake, in western Ontario. The moth may be collected in May.

Cucullia speyeri Lintner

Fig. 238

The CNC has specimens of this species from Ontario, from Queenston to Trenton. The larva feeds on Canada fleabane (*Erigeron canadensis* L.). The adult may be collected in June.

Cucullia intermedia Speyer

Fig. 239

This species is common across both Ontario and Quebec as far north as North Bay. The adult may be collected from early June until late August. The larva feeds on wild lettuce (*Lactuca* spp.).

Cucullia florea Guenée

Fig. 240

This species is found in Ontario from Hymers to Smoky Falls and Ottawa, and in Quebec from St. Sauveur and Knowlton. The adult may be collected during June and July.

Cucullia postera Guenée

Fig. 242

This primarily western species has been collected in eastern Ontario. The moth may be collected in July. The larva feeds on wild aster (*Aster* spp.), possibly on the flowers.

Cucullia omissa Dod

Fig. 234

The CNC has specimens of this species from Black Sturgeon Lake, Ogoki, and Ottawa, Ont. There is no material from Quebec in the CNC. The food plant is aster (*Aster* spp.). The adult may be collected in July.

Cucullia asteroides Guenée

Fig. 243

This species is very similar to *C. omissa* but the hind wing is much paler. It is found in southern and eastern Ontario, and also from Norway Bay to Forestville, Que. The moth may be collected from the end of May until August. The larva feeds on the flowers of aster (*Aster* spp.) and goldenrod (*Solidago* spp.).

Cucullia convexipennis Grote & Robinson

Fig. 244

This species is found in southern and eastern Ontario from Simcoe to Ottawa. There are no specimens from Quebec in the CNC. The moth may be collected in late July and August. The larva feeds on aster (*Aster* spp.) and goldenrod (*Solidago* spp.), preferring the flowers.

Oncocnemis saundersiana Grote

Fig. 245

The specimens of this species in the CNC are from southern and eastern Ontario. They were all reared on beardtongue (*Penstemon* spp.). The adult may be collected in late August and early September: it is not common.

Oncocnemis piffardi (Walker)

Fig. 246

This species is rare in collections; the CNC has material from Sault Ste. Marie and Smoky Falls, Ont., and from Forestville and Laniel, Que. The adult occurs in August.

Oncocnemis riparia Morrison

Fig. 247

The CNC has material of this species from Grand Bend and Port Colborne, in southern Ontario. There are no specimens from Quebec in the CNC. The moth may be collected from late June until mid-July.

Homohadena badistriga (Grote)

Fig. 248

This species is found across the central and southern region of Ontario and western Quebec. The larva feeds on honeysuckle (*Lonicera* spp.). The adult may be collected in late June and July.

Homohadena infixa (Walker)

Fig. 252

This species is common in Western Canada and has been collected as far east as eastern Ontario. The adult may be collected in July.

Adita chionanthi (J. E. Smith)

Fig. 249

This primarily western species has been collected in the Georgian Bay district and in southeastern Ontario. There is no material from Quebec in the CNC. The moth may be collected in late August and September. Black ash (*Fraxinus nigra* Marsh.) is the food plant of the larva.

Apharetra purpurea McDunnough

Fig. 250

This species is found in the central regions of both Ontario and Quebec, from Mer Bleue, near Ottawa, northward to Larder Lake, Ont., and from Laniel eastward to Forestville, Que. The larva feeds on blueberry (*Vaccinium* spp.). The adult may be collected in late July and August.

Sympistis melaleuca (Thunberg)

Fig. 254

This alpine species has been collected at Fort Chimo and Knob Lake, in northern Quebec, and also at Mt. Albert, in the Gaspé Peninsula. The larva feeds on crowberry (*Empetrum* spp.). The moth may be collected in July.

Sympistis lapponica (Thunberg)

Fig. 255

The adult is similar to *S. melaleuca*. This species has been collected at Payne Bay and Port Harrison, in northern Quebec, during August. The larva feeds on blueberry (*Vaccinium* spp.).

Sympistis labradoris (Staudinger)

Fig. 253

The CNC has material of this species from Payne Bay and Port Harrison, in northern Quebec. The moth may be collected in July. The larva feeds on dryas (*Dryas* spp.).

Sympistis kolthoffi (Aurivillius)

Fig. 257

The only representatives of this species in the CNC are from Cape Henrietta Maria, Ont., at the top of James Bay. The adult occurs in July.

Sympistis funesta (Paykull)

Fig. 251

The CNC has representatives of this northern species from Mistassini Post and Sept Iles, Que. The moth may be collected in July.

Feralia jocosa (Guenée)

Fig. 261

This species has been found in Ontario from Lindsay eastward to Ottawa and in western Quebec at Harrington Lake. The adult may be collected in April and early May. The larva feeds on spruce (*Picea* spp.) and eastern hemlock (*Tsuga canadensis* (L.) Carr.).

Feralia major Smith

Fig. 262

This uncommon species has been collected at Toronto, Ottawa, and Hull. The larva feeds on spruce (*Picea* spp.). The moth occurs in April and May.

Feralia comstocki Grote

Fig. 263

This species is found across both Ontario and Quebec from Black Sturgeon Lake eastward to Mt. Lyall. The larva feeds on eastern hemlock (*Tsuga canadensis* (L.) Carr.). The adult may be collected in May.

Copivaleria grotei (Morrison)

Fig. 264

The CNC has representatives of this species from southern and eastern Ontario and Kirk's Ferry, in western Quebec. The moth may be collected during May and June. The larva feeds on ash (*Fraxinus* spp.).

Psaphida thaxteriana (Grote)

Fig. 265

The only record for Canada of this species is one from Delhi, in southern Ontario. The adult occurs in early May. The larva feeds on oak (*Quercus* spp.).

A similar species, *Psaphida resumens* Walker, with a thick black dash on the outer edge of the fore wing, has recently been collected in southern and eastern Ontario in late April and early May.

Eutolype rolandi Grote

Fig. 258

The only specimens of this species in the CNC are from Chatham, in southern Ontario and Chaffey's Locks in eastern Ontario. The moth occurs in late March and April.

Copipanolis styracis (Guenée)

Fig. 259

The only specimens of this species in the CNC are from London and Pembroke, Ont. The adult occurs in April. The larva feeds on oak (*Quercus* spp.).

Bombycia algens (Grote)

Fig. 266

This species is found across Ontario from Hymers eastward to Larder Lake and Ottawa. The moth may be collected in late July and August.

Brachylomia discinigra (Walker)

Fig. 267

The CNC has representatives of this species from Ogoki, Ont., and Forestville, Que. The adult may be collected in August.

Hillia iris (Zetterstedt)

Fig. 260

This species is common across northern Canada and has been found at Ogoki, Ont., and in the Ottawa Valley. The adult may be collected in August and September.

Lemmeria digitalis (Grote)

Fig. 273

This species has been found at Coldstream and Manotick, Ont. The adult occurs in September and October; it is not common.

Litholomia napaea (Morrison)

Fig. 268

This species has been found from Hymers, Ont., eastward to Norway Bay and Meach Lake, in western Quebec. The larva feeds on trembling aspen (*Populus tremuloides* Michx.). The moth may be collected in September and October.

Lithomoia solidaginis (Hübner)

Fig. 269

This species is found across the central regions of both Ontario and Quebec between the 45th and 50th parallels. The moth may be collected in late August and September. The larva feeds on blueberry (*Vaccinium* spp.) and Labrador tea (*Ledum groenlandicum* Oeder).

Lithophane semiusta Grote

Fig. 279

The CNC has material of this species from southern and eastern Ontario and from Lac Mondor, Que. The adult may be collected in September and in April. Species in the genus *Lithophane* overwinter as adults. The larva feeds on basswood (*Tilia americana* L.) and red choke cherry (*Prunus virginiana* L.).

Lithophane patefacta (Walker)

Fig. 280

This species has been found in southern and eastern Ontario, and in the Montreal region. The larva feeds on red choke cherry (*Prunus virginiana* L.). The moth may be collected in September and in May.

Lithophane bethunei (Grote & Robinson)

Fig. 281

This species is fairly common in the southern part of both Ontario and Quebec from London eastward to Lac Mondor. The larva feeds on most deciduous trees and has been reared on ash (*Fraxinus jt5spp.*), elm (*Ulmus* spp.), maple (*Acer* spp.), beech *Fagus grandifolia* Ehrh.), and red choke cherry (*Prunus virginiana* L.). The adult may be collected in September and in early May.

Lithophane innominata (Smith)

Fig. 282

This species is found across central and southern Ontario and Quebec from Hymers, in northwestern Ontario, eastward to Lac Mondor, Que. The adult may be collected in September and in early May. Red choke cherry (*Prunus virginiana* L.) is the food plant of the larva.

Lithophane petulca Grote

Figs. 283, 284

This species is found throughout the central and southern regions of Ontario and Quebec from Black Sturgeon Lake, Ont., eastward to Laurentide Park, Que. The moth may be collected in September and in early May. The larva has been reared on red choke cherry (*Prunus virginiana* L.).

Lithophane amanda (Smith)

Fig. 285

This species is found in the central regions of Ontario and Quebec from Smoky Falls eastward to Ottawa and Laurentide Park. The moth may be collected in September and in May.

Lithophane disposita Morrison

Fig. 286

This species occurs from London eastward to Ottawa and Lac Mondor, Que. The adult may be collected in September and in April and May. The larva feeds on red choke cherry (*Prunus virginiana* L.) and willow (*Salix* spp.).

Lithophane hemina Grote

Fig. 287

This species is found from London eastward to Ottawa and at Meach Lake, in western Quebec. The moth may be collected in September and in early May. The larva has been reared on red choke cherry (*Prunus virginiana* L.).

Lithophane oriunda Grote

Fig. 293

This uncommon species has been collected in southern and eastern Ontario and in southern Quebec. The adult may be collected in September and in early May. This species has been reared on red choke cherry (*Prunus virginiana* L.).

Lithophane baileyi Grote

Fig. 289

This species has been found across the central regions of both Ontario and Quebec from Hymers eastward to Ottawa and Lac Mondor, Que. The larva feeds on red choke cherry (*Prunus virginiana* L.). The moth may be collected in September and in April.

Lithophane tepida Grote

Fig. 271

This uncommon species has been collected in central and eastern Ontario and in Quebec at New Carlisle, in the Gaspé Peninsula. The adult may be collected in September.

Lithophane antennata (Walker)

Fig. 290

The CNC has material of this species from southern and eastern Ontario and southern Quebec. The moth may be collected in September and in early May. The larva, commonly called the green fruitworm, feeds on apple (*Pyrus* spp.), and occasionally damages the young fruit.

Lithophane georgii Grote

Fig. 291

This species is found from Black Sturgeon Lake eastward to Ottawa and to Lac Mondor, Que. The larva feeds on apple (*Pyrus* spp.), alder (*Alnus* spp.), and raspberry (*Rubus* spp.). The adult may be collected in October and in April.

Lithophane laticinerea Grote

Fig. 292

This species is found across the southern regions of both Ontario and Quebec from London eastward to Ottawa and to Lac Mondor, Que. The moth may be collected in September and in early May. The larva feeds on red choke cherry (*Prunus virginiana* L.) and apple (*Pyrus* spp.).

Lithophane grotei Riley

Fig. 288

This species has been found in eastern Ontario and southern Quebec. The moth may be collected in October and April.

Lithophane unimoda (Lintner)

Fig. 294

The species is prevalent across the central and southern regions of both Ontario and Quebec from Black Sturgeon Lake eastward to Ottawa and to Lac Mondor, Que. The moth may be collected in September and in May. The larva feeds on black cherry (*Prunus serotina* Ehrh.) and red choke cherry (*Prunus virginiana* L.).

Lithophane fagina Morrison

Fig. 295

This species has been collected across the central and southern regions of both Ontario and Quebec from Black Sturgeon Lake eastward to Lac Mondor, Que. The adult may be collected in September and in May. The larva feeds on white birch (*Betula papyrifera* Marsh.).

Lithophane pexata Grote

Fig. 296

This species occurs throughout Ontario and Quebec as far north as the 50th parallel. The adult may be collected in September and in May. The larva feeds on alder (*Alnus* spp.).

Lithophane lepida (Lintner)

Fig. 297

This uncommon species has been collected from Fort Frances, in western Ontario, eastward to southern Quebec. The larva feeds on red pine (*Pinus resinosa* Ait.). The moth occurs in September and in April.

Lithophane lamda thaxteri Grote

Fig. 272

This species has been collected in Ontario at Hymers and Ottawa. The larva feeds on New Jersey tea (*Ceanothus* spp.). The adult may be collected in October and April.

Xylena nupera (Lintner)

Fig. 298

This species is found across the central and southern regions of both Ontario and Quebec from Hymers eastward to Ottawa and Lac Mondor. The larva feeds on cherry (*Prunus* spp.) and poplar (*Populus* spp.). The moth may be collected in September and May.

Xylena curvimacula (Morrison)

Fig. 299

This species is found throughout the central and southern regions of both Ontario and Quebec from Black Sturgeon Lake eastward to Lac Mondor. The larva feeds on alder (*Alnus* spp.), poplar (*Populus* spp.), and red choke cherry (*Prunus virginiana* L.). The moth may be collected in September and in May overwintering as an adult.

Xylena thoracica (Putnam-Cramer)

Fig. 300

This species is found across the north central part of Ontario and Quebec from Hymers and Smoky Falls, Ont., eastward through the Abitibi region to Rimouski, Que. The adult may be collected in September and in April; it overwinters as an adult.

Xylena cineritia (Grote)

Fig. 270

This species is found in Ontario from Hymers eastward to Smoky Falls and southward to Kingston. The adult may be collected in September and in April; it overwinters as an adult.

Xylotype acadia Barnes & Benjamin

Fig. 301

This species is found across the north central regions of both Ontario and Quebec from Ogoki eastward to Laurentide Park. The adult may be collected in August. The larva feeds on tamarack (*Larix laricina* (Du Roi) K. Koch).

Platypolia anceps (Stephens)

Fig. 302

This species is found throughout the central regions of both Ontario and Quebec from Hymers eastward to Laurentide Park and southward to Ottawa. The moth may be collected in September.

Mniotype ducta (Grote)

Fig. 303

This species has been collected in Quebec from Knowlton eastward to Percé, at the tip of the Gaspé Peninsula. No specimens have been collected from Ontario. The moth may be collected in June and July.

Mniotype versuta (Smith)

Fig. 274

This species is more common in Western Canada. Three specimens in the CNC were collected from Smoky Falls, in northern Ontario, in June.

Mniotype miniota (Smith)

Fig. 304

The CNC has specimens of this species from Thunder Bay eastward to Smoky Falls in northern Ontario. There is no material from Quebec in the CNC. The adult may be collected in June and July.

Fishia enthea Grote

Fig. 305

This species has been collected in central and eastern Ontario from Hymers to Sudbury and southward to Kingston. There is no material from Quebec in the CNC. This uncommon species may be collected in September.

Sutyna privata (Walker)

Fig. 306

This species occurs throughout southern and eastern Ontario and eastward to Granby, Que. The adult may be collected in August and September.

Sutyna profunda (Smith)

Fig. 307

This species is found across the central regions of both Ontario and Quebec from Hymers northward to Ogoki and eastward to Laurentide Park. The adult may be collected in August and September.

Chaetaglaea sericea (Morrison)

Fig. 275

The CNC has specimens from eastern Ontario. The larva has been reared on red choke cherry (*Prunus virginiana* L.) and black cherry (*Prunus serotina* Ehrh.). The adult occurs from September to November.

Psectraglaea carnosa (Grote)

Fig. 308

This species is found from London northward to Sault Ste. Marie and eastward to Joliette, Que. The moth may be fairly common in sandy areas where the host plants occur. The moth may be collected in October. Blueberry (*Vaccinium* spp.) and oak (*Quercus* spp.) are the hosts of the larva.

Epiglaea decliva (Grote)

Fig. 309

The only records of this species from Ontario in the CNC are from the vicinities of London and Kingston. The larva feeds on black cherry (*Prunus serotina* Ehrh.) and red choke cherry (*Prunus virginiana* L.). The adult occurs in September and October.

Epiglaea apiata (Grote)

Fig. 310

This species has been collected in the central part of Ontario and Quebec from Timmins eastward to Lac Mondor and southward to Ottawa. The species is common in the Mer Bleue bog, near Ottawa. The larva feeds on cranberry and blueberry (*Vaccinium* spp.). The adult may be collected in late August and September.

Metaxaglaea inulta (Grote)

Fig. 311

The CNC has material of this species from Port Colborne eastward to

Ottawa and Lac Mondor, Que. The moth may be collected in September. Arrowwood (*Viburnum* spp.) is the food plant of the larva.

Pyreferra indirecta (Walker)

Fig. 312

This species is represented in the CNC by specimens from the vicinity of Hamilton and Long Point, Ont. The larva feeds on witch-hazel (*Hamamelis virginiana* L.). The adult may be collected in September and in early May. Species in the genus *Pyreferra* overwinter as adults.

Pyreferra citromba Franclemont

Figs. 276, 313

The CNC has material of this species from western Ontario eastward to Montreal. The adult may be collected in September and in May. The larva feeds on hazel (*Corylus* spp.).

Pyreferra pettiti (Grote)

Fig. 314

This species is found from southern Ontario eastward to Lac Mondor, Que. The larva feeds on cherry birch (*Betula lenta* L.) and yellow birch (*Betula alleghaniensis* Britton). The adult may be collected in September and in May.

Pyreferra ceromatica (Grote)

Fig. 315

The CNC has representatives of this species from the Toronto–Hamilton area. There is no material from Quebec in the CNC. The moth may be collected in April. The larva feeds on witch-hazel (*Hamamelis virginiana* L.).

Eupsilia tristigmata (Grote)

Fig. 316

This species occurs in the southern and central parts of Ontario and Quebec as far north as Hymers, Sudbury, and Lac Mondor. The moth may be collected in September and in early May. Species in the genus *Eupsilia* overwinter as adults. The larva feeds on cherry (*Prunus* spp.).

Eupsilia vinulenta (Grote)

Fig. 317

This species is found from London to Ottawa, Ont., and Lac Mondor, Que.

The adult may be collected in August and in May.

Eupsilia morrisoni (Grote)

Fig. 318

This species occurs from London, Ont., eastward to Lac Mondor, Que. The larva feeds on white elm (*Ulmus americana* L.), maple (*Acer* spp.), and cherry (*Prunus* spp.). The moth may be collected in October and in May.

Eupsilia devia (Grote)

Fig. 319

Although this species is widespread in Canada, the only material in the CNC from Ontario and Quebec was collected in the vicinities of Ottawa and Montreal. The larva feeds on goldenrod (*Solidago* spp.), aster (*Aster* spp.), and red choke cherry (*Prunus virginiana* L.). The moth may be collected in October and May.

Parastichtis discivaria (Walker)

Fig. 320

This species is common across the central regions of both Ontario and Quebec from the Manitoba border eastward to Forestville and southward to London and Ottawa. The adult may be collected in August.

Sunira bicolorago (Guenée)

Fig. 321

This common species occurs from London, Ont., eastward to Laurentide Park, Que. The larva feeds on dock (*Rumex* spp.) and tobacco (*Nicotiana* spp.). The adult may be collected in September and October.

Xanthia lutea (Ström)

Fig. 322

This species is common in the central and southern parts of Ontario and Quebec as far north as Black Sturgeon Lake and Lac Mondor. The larva feeds on willow (*Salix* spp.), preferring the catkins. The moth may be collected during September.

Anathix ralla (Grote)

Fig. 323

This species is found from southern Ontario eastward to Ottawa and Montreal. The adult may be collected in late August and September.

Anathix puta (Grote & Robinson)

Fig. 324

This species is common throughout Ontario and Quebec as far north as James Bay. The larva feeds on trembling aspen (*Populus tremuloides* Michx.). The moth may be collected in August.

Eucirrhoedia pampina (Guenée)

Fig. 325

This species is represented in the CNC by material from the central and southern regions of Ontario and Quebec from Black Sturgeon Lake eastward to Lac Mondor. The larva feeds on red choke cherry (*Prunus virginiana* L.), black cherry (*Prunus serotina* Ehrh.), and maple (*Acer* spp.). The moth may be collected in September.

Homoglaea hircina Morrison

Fig. 332

This species has been collected from Trenton, Ont., eastward to Lac Mondor, Que. The larva feeds on trembling aspen (*Populus tremuloides* Michx.). The moth may be collected in October, April, and May; it overwinters as an adult.

Subfamily Amphipyrinae

The subfamily Amphipyrinae is made up of about 90 genera and 385 species. The main characters of the Amphipyrinae are the unlashed and naked eyes of the moths, and the lack of spines on the tibia.

Apamea verbascoides Guenée)

Fig. 327

This species is found in the central and southern part of both Ontario and Quebec from Black Sturgeon Lake eastward to Knowlton and Forestville. The moth may be collected in June and July.

Apamea nigrior (Smith)

Fig. 328

This species is represented in the CNC by material from southern and eastern Ontario. There are no specimens from Quebec in the CNC. The adult may be collected in June.

Apamea cariosa (Guenée)

Fig. 329

This species has been collected in southern and eastern Ontario, and in western Quebec. The moth may be collected in July.

Apamea lignicolora (Guenée)

Fig. 330

This species is common across Ontario and Quebec from Windsor eastward to Lac Mondor. The larva feeds on grasses (Gramineae). The adult may be collected in June and July.

Apamea vultuosa (Grote)

Fig. 331

This species is common in both Ontario and Quebec from Black Sturgeon Lake eastward to Forestville and as far north as Ogoki. The larva feeds on various kinds of grasses (Gramineae). The adult may be collected in June and July.

Apamea apamiformis (Guenée)

Fig. 326

This species is widespread in Ontario from Hymers eastward to Ottawa. There are no specimens from Quebec in the CNC. The larva feeds on wild-rice (*Zizania aquatica* L.). Heavy infestations of this species severely damage the wild-rice plants. The eggs are oviposited inside the florets of the plant. The moth may be collected in July.

Apamea plutonia (Grote)

Fig. 277

Although this species is probably widespread in Ontario, the CNC has only two specimens, one from Hymers and the other from Ottawa. The moth may be collected in late June and July, but apparently it is not common.

Apamea amputatrix (Fitch)

Fig. 333

This species is common throughout Ontario and Quebec as far north as the 50th parallel. The larva is commonly called the yellowheaded cutworm. The moth may be collected from June until August.

Apamea alia (Guenée)

Fig. 334

This species is found as far north as Black Sturgeon Lake and Ogoki in Ontario and Sept Iles in Quebec. The larva feeds on grasses (Gramineae). The adult may be collected in June and July.

Apamea inordinata (Morrison)

Fig. 278

The CNC has specimens of this species only from southern and eastern Ontario. The adult occurs in June.

Apamea commoda (Walker)

Fig. 338

This species is found across the central regions of both Ontario and Quebec from Hymers eastward to Mistassini Post and southward to Sudbury. The adult may be collected in June, July, and August.

Apamea impulsa (Guenée)

Fig. 336

The CNC has material of this species from Black Sturgeon Lake, Ont., eastward to Kamouraska County, in the Gaspé Peninsula, and as far south as Trenton, Ont. The moth may be collected in June and July.

Apamea mixta (Grote)

Fig. 337

This species is represented in the CNC by a specimen from Westree, in the central region of Ontario. The adult may be collected in August.

Apamea indocilis (Walker)

Fig. 335

This species is widespread in both Ontario and Quebec from Ogoki, Ont., eastward to Mt. Lyall, in the Gaspé Peninsula, and as far south as Trenton, Ont. The larva feeds on grasses (Gramineae). The adult may be collected in June and July.

Apamea finitima Guenée

Fig. 339

This species is fairly common from southern Ontario eastward to the Gaspé Peninsula in Quebec. The larva feeds on wheat (*Elymus* spp.), wild-rice (*Zizania aquatica* L.), timothy (*Phleum* spp.), and corn (*Zea mays* L.). The adult may be collected in June and July.

Agroperina lateritia (Hufnagel)

Fig. 340

This species is prevalent throughout both Ontario and Quebec, from the Manitoba border eastward to Labrador. The moth may be collected in late June and July.

Agroperina dubitans (Walker)

Fig. 341

This species is common in the southern half of Ontario and Quebec, as far north as Ogoki, Ont., and the Gaspé Peninsula, Que. The larva feeds on grasses (Gramineae). The moth may be collected in July and August.

Agroperina cogitata (Smith)

Fig. 342

This species is abundant across both Ontario and Quebec as far north as Ogoki and Mistassini Post. The adult may be collected in July.

Agroperina inficita (Walker)

Fig. 378

This species is represented in the CNC by material from Bradore Bay, in the eastermost part of Quebec, and Cascapedia, in the Gaspé Peninsula. The adult may be collected in August.

Agroperina lutosa (Andrews)

Fig. 343

The CNC has material of this species from the Chatham area, in southern Ontario, and from Montreal. The moth may be collected in July.

Agroperina helva (Grote)

Fig. 344

The CNC has material of this species from eastern Ontario and from Lac Mondor, Que. The larva feeds on sod. The moth may be collected in late July and August.

Crymodes devastator (Brace)

Fig. 345

This species is common throughout both Ontario and Quebec. The larva, commonly called the glassy cutworm, feeds on grass and may sometimes cause serious damage. The moth may be collected during July and August.

Trichoplexia exornata (Möschler)

Fig. 346

This northern species has been found from Black Sturgeon Lake, Ont., eastward to Labrador. The moth may be collected in late June and July.

Protagrotis niveivenosa (Grote)

Fig. 347

This species is found across Ontario and Quebec as far north as Black Sturgeon Lake and Lac Mondor. The adult may be collected in July.

Protagrotis extensa (Smith)

Fig. 379

There is only one specimen of this species in the CNC from Ottawa. The moth occurs in July and August.

Luperina stipata (Morrison)

Fig. 380

Like many borers, this species is uncommon and has only been found at Meach Lake, in western Quebec. The larva bores in the stalks of grasses (Gramineae). The adult occurs in late July.

Luperina obtusa (Smith)

Fig. 381

This species has been collected at Port Colborne, in southern Ontario, during July and August.

Luperina passer (Guenée)

Fig. 348

This species has been collected in southern and eastern Ontario. There is no material from Quebec in the CNC. The moth may be collected in July and August. The larva feeds on the roots of dock (*Rumex* spp.).

Oligia modica (Guenée)

Fig. 349

This species has been collected in southern and eastern Ontario and at Lac la Tortue, near Grand Mère, Que. The moth may be collected during July and August.

Oligia semicana (Walker)

Fig. 350

The only specimens from Ontario or Quebec in the CNC were collected in eastern Ontario and at Norway Bay, in western Quebec. The adult may be collected in June and July.

Oligia exhausta (Smith)

Fig. 382

Specimens of this species were collected in southeastern Ontario and at Montreal. The moth occurs in June and July.

Oligia bridghami (Grote & Robinson)

Fig. 351

This species is represented in the CNC by specimens from Ottawa and Sudbury, Ont. The adult may be collected in late July and August.

Oligia minuscula (Morrison)

Fig. 352

The CNC has material of this species from peat bogs in eastern Ontario. The moth occurs in late August and early September. It is very local and not common.

Oligia diversicolor (Morrison)

Fig. 353

This species occurs from southern Ontario eastward to western Quebec and northward to Sudbury, Ont. The adult may be collected in August. The larva bores into the stems of sedges (Cyperaceae).

Oligia illocata (Walker)

Fig. 354

This species occurs across the central and southern regions of both Ontario and Quebec from Black Sturgeon Lake, in western Ontario, eastward to Laurentide Park, Que. The moth may be collected in late August and September. The larva feeds on birch (*Betula* spp.) and alder (*Alnus* spp.).

Oligia mactata (Guenée)

Fig. 355

This species is found in Ontario from Hymers eastward to Ottawa and in western Quebec from Meach Lake northward to Laniel. The adult may be collected in late August and September.

Oligia fractilinea (Grote)

Fig. 356

This species is represented in the CNC by material from eastern Ontario and western Quebec. The larva, commonly called the lined stalk borer, is occasionally a pest on young corn, but usually it bores in other grasses. The moth may be collected during August.

Eremobina claudens (Walker)

Fig. 357

This species has been collected only at Ogoki, in northern Ontario. There are no specimens from Quebec in the CNC. The moth may be collected in August.

Eremobina jocasta (Smith)

Fig. 358

The CNC has material of this species from southern and eastern Ontario. The adult may be collected in August and September.

Xylomoia chagnoni Barnes & McDunnough

Fig. 359

This uncommon species is found in southern and eastern Ontario and in southern Quebec. The adult occurs in July and August. The larva bores in reed canary grass (*Phalaris arundinacea* L.).

Spartiniphaga includens (Walker)

Fig. 360

This species has been collected from southern Ontario eastward to Trenton. The moth may be collected in July.

Spartiniphaga panatela (Smith)

Fig. 361

This species occurs from southern and eastern Ontario northward to Sudbury. The moth may be collected in June.

Archanara oblonga (Grote)

Fig. 383

The larva of this species bores in the stalks of cattails (*Typha* spp.). The moth has been collected in eastern Ontario and at Montreal. The adult may be collected in September.

Archanara subflava (Grote)

Fig. 362

This species is found in Ontario from Hymers eastward to Kingston. There are no specimens from Quebec in the CNC. The larva bores in grasses (Gramineae). The moth may be collected from July until September.

Archanara laeta (Morrison)

Fig. 363

The only specimens of this rare species in the CNC are from the Mer Bleue bog, near Ottawa, Brockville, Ont., and from Granby, Que. The larva feeds on bur-reed (*Sparganium* spp.). The adult may be collected from June until August.

Hypocoena rufostrigata (Packard)

Fig. 364

This species is represented in the CNC by material from Bradore Bay, Que. There are no specimens from Ontario in the CNC. The adult occurs in July.

Hypocoena inquinata (Guenée)

Fig. 384

This species is found from Strathroy, in southern Ontario, eastward to Ottawa and Laniel, in western Quebec. The adult may be collected in late July and early August.

Senta defecta Grote

Fig. 365

This species has been collected in Ontario from Chatham and Thunder Bay eastward. There is no material from Quebec in the CNC. The moth is rare; it occurs in July.

Ipimorpha pleonectusa Grote

Fig. 366

This common species occurs across central and southern Ontario and Quebec from Ogoki eastward to Lac Mondor. The larva feeds on trembling aspen (*Populus tremuloides* Michx.). The adult may be collected in July and August.

Helotropha reniformis (Grote)

Fig. 367

This species occurs across central and southern Ontario and Quebec from Black Sturgeon Lake eastward to Lac Mondor. Occasionally the larva may damage corn, but usually it feeds on sedges (Cyperaceae). The moth may be collected in August and September.

Amphipoea velata (Walker)

Fig. 368

This species has been collected from Hymers, in western Ontario, southward to Lake Ontario, and eastward to Forestville, on the north shore of the St. Lawrence River. The moth may be collected in July and August. The larva feeds on grasses (Gramineae).

Amphipoea americana (Speyer)

Fig. 369

This species is common across both Ontario and Quebec as far north as Ogoki and Forestville. The larva is a minor pest of young corn. The adult may be collected in August and September.

Amphipoea interoceanica (Smith)

Fig. 370

This species is represented in the CNC by material from southern and eastern Ontario. There are no specimens from Quebec in the CNC. The moth may be collected in July. Often difficult to distinguish from preceding species by external markings but pale portion of reniform spot confined to outer two-thirds of spot. In *americana* some pale shading extends to the inner edge of spot.

Hydroecia immanis Guenée

Fig. 371

The CNC has specimens from only eastern Ontario and western Quebec. The adult may be collected in September. The larva is a minor pest of hops (*Humulus* spp.).

Hydroecia micacea (Esper)

Fig. 385

The larva of this species, commonly called the potato stem borer, is sometimes a moderate pest on potatoes and corn. The moth has been collected from eastern Ontario eastward to the Gaspé Peninsula of Quebec. The adult may be collected during August.

Hydroecia stramentosa Guenée

Fig. 372

This species has been collected only in the Ottawa and Montreal regions. The moth occurs in late August and September; it is not common.

Papaipema cerina (Grote)

Fig. 373

The CNC has representatives of this species from Delhi, in southern Ontario. The larva bores in the stems of lilies (*Lilium* spp.) and the mayapple (*Podophyllum peltatum* L.). The adult may be collected in late September and October.

Papaipema appassionata (Harvey)

Fig. 374

This species is found in peat bogs where its larval host, the pitcherplant

(*Sarracenia purpurea* L.), occurs. The CNC has material from peat bogs in eastern Ontario. The moth may be collected in late August and September.

Papaipema inquaesita (Grote & Robinson)

Fig. 375

This species has been collected from southern Ontario to western Quebec. The larva bores in the stems of sensitive fern (*Onoclea sensibilis* L.). The moth may be collected in September.

Papaipema marginidens (Guenée)

Fig. 376

This species bores in bulbous water-hemlock (*Cicuta bulbifera* L.) and has been collected from Trenton to Brockville in eastern Ontario. There is no material from Quebec in the CNC. The adult may be collected in late August and September.

Papaipema nepheleptena (Dyar)

Fig. 377

This species has been found in southern and eastern Ontario. The larva bores in the stems of turtlehead (*Chelone glabra* L.). The moth may be collected in October.

Papaipema furcata (Smith)

Fig. 387

The CNC has specimens of this species, from eastern Ontario and southern Quebec. The larva bores in the terminal twigs of ash (*Fraxinus* spp.). The adult occurs in September.

Papaipema arctivorens Hampson

Fig. 388

This species has been found at Ancaster, in southern Ontario, and at Montreal. The larva bores in common burdock (*Arctium minus* (Hill) Bernh.), Canada thistle *Cirsium arvense* (L.) Scop.), and teasel (*Dipsacus sylvestris* Huds.). The moth may be collected in late August and September.

Papaipema harrisii (Grote)

Fig. 389

This species has been found from Hymers eastward to Toronto, Ottawa, and Montreal. The adult may be collected in September. The larva bores in the stems of cow-parsnip (*Heracleum lanatum* Michx.) and angelica (*Angelica* spp.).

Papaipema impecuniosa (Grote)

Fig. 390

This species has been collected in southern and eastern Ontario. The larva bores in the stems of aster (*Aster* spp.) and sneezeweed (*Helenium* spp.). The moth may be collected in late September and October.

Papaipema purpurifascia (Grote & Robinson)

Fig. 391

The larva of this species, commonly called the columbine borer, is sometimes a pest of gardens. The CNC has material from Port Colborne eastward to Ottawa. The adult may be collected in late August and September.

Papaipema lysimachiae Bird

Fig. 392

The CNC has specimens of this species from eastern Ontario. The larva bores in the stems of loosestrife (*Lysimachia* spp.). The moth occurs in September.

Papaipema pterisii Bird

Fig. 393

This species is common across the central regions of Ontario and Quebec from Hymers, in northwestern Ontario, to Lac Mondor, Que., and southward to Ottawa and Montreal. The moth may be collected during September. The larva bores in the stems of bracken (*Pteridium aquilinum* (L.) Kuhn).

Papaipema cataphracta (Grote)

Fig. 394

This species occurs commonly from southern Ontario eastward to western Quebec. The larva, commonly called the burdock borer, bores in the stems of burdock (*Arctium* spp.). The moth may be collected in September.

Papaipema duovata (Bird)

Fig. 386

The CNC has only one specimen from eastern Ontario. The moth occurs in late September and early October. The larva feeds on goldenrod (*Solidago* spp.).

Papaipema aweme (Lyman)

Fig. 414

The CNC has one specimen from Grand Bend, Ont. It was collected in August.

Papaipema nelita (Strecker)

Fig. 415

The CNC has a specimen reared from a larva found boring in the stem of burdock (*Arctium* spp.), at Stittsville, Ont. The adult may be collected in late August and September.

Papaipema frigida (Smith)

Fig. 395

This species is found across the central and southern regions of both Ontario and Quebec from Hymers eastward to Lac Mondor. The larva bores in meadow-rue (*Thalictrum* spp.) and coneflower (*Rudbeckia* spp.). The adult may be collected in late September.

Papaipema limpida (Guenée)

Fig. 416

This species is represented in the CNC by a specimen from Montreal. The larva bores in the stems of burdock (*Arctium* spp.). The moth may be collected in August.

Papaipema eupatorii (Lyman)

Fig. 417

This species has been collected in eastern Ontario and at Beauport, Que. The adult occurs in late August and September. The larva bores in the stems of Joe-Pye weed (*Eupatorium purpureum* L.).

Euplexia benesimilis McDunnough

Fig. 396

This species is found throughout both Ontario and Quebec as far north as James Bay. The larva has been reared on arrowwood (*Viburnum* spp.). The adult may be collected during June and July.

Phlogophora iris Guenée

Fig. 397

This species is common throughout both Ontario and Quebec as far north as James Bay. The larva has been reared on sensitive fern (*Onoclea sensibilis* L.). The adult may be collected in June and July.

Phlogophora periculosa Guenée

Fig. 398

This species is common across both Ontario and Quebec as far north as James Bay. The larva feeds on alder (*Alnus* spp.), blueberry (*Vaccinium* spp.), wild plum (*Prunus americana* Marsh.), and balsam fir (*Abies balsamea* (L.) Mill.). The adult may be collected during August and September.

Conservula anodonta (Guenée)

Fig. 399

This species is found in acid bogs in eastern and central Ontario and southern and western Quebec. The restricted habitat may be the reason for its apparent scarcity. The moth occurs during July and August.

Haploolophus mollissima (Guenée)

Fig. 400

This species has been collected from Trenton, Ont., eastward to Lac Mondor, Que. The adult may be collected in June and July.

Euherrichia monetifera (Guenée)

Fig. 401

This species occurs throughout both Ontario and Quebec as far north as Lake Nipigon and Forestville. The larva feeds on sensitive fern (*Onoclea sensibilis* L.). The moth may be collected in June and July.

Fagitana littera (Guenée)

Fig. 418

This species is considered to be rare and sporadic. The CNC has only one specimen from Ottawa, which was collected in June. Marsh-fern (*Thelypteris palustris* Schott) is the food plant.

Macronoctua onusta Grote

Fig. 402

This species occurs from southern Ontario eastward to Ottawa, and to Granby, Que. The larva, commonly called the iris borer, bores in the roots of iris (*Iris* spp.). The moth may be collected in September. The adult is rarely obtained except by rearing.

Trachea delicata (Grote)

Fig. 403

The CNC has material of this species from Port Colborne eastward to Ottawa. The adult may be collected in late June and July.

Chytonix palliatricula (Guenée)

Fig. 404

This species is found from southern Ontario eastward to Forestville, Que. The moth may be collected during June and July.

Chytonix sensilis Grote

Fig. 405

This species is found in southern and eastern Ontario and at Norway Bay, in western Quebec. The adult may be collected in July.

Cerma cora Hübner

Fig. 406

This rare species has been collected in southern and eastern Ontario. There is no material of this species from Quebec in the CNC. The larva feeds on pin cherry (*Prunus pensylvania* L.f.). The adult occurs in June.

Polygrammate hebraeicum Hübner

Fig. 419

This species has been collected at Normandale and Vittoria, in southern

Ontario, where the species is common in localized areas. There is no material from Quebec in the CNC. The moth may be collected in mid-July. The larva feeds on black gum (*Nyssa sylvatica* Marsh.).

Leuconycta diphteroides (Guenée)

Fig. 407

This species is found in southern and eastern Ontario and in Quebec as far east as Lac Mondor. The larva has been reared on goldenrod (*Solidago* spp.). The moth may be collected in June.

Leuconycta lepidula (Grote)

Fig. 408

This species has been found in central and eastern Ontario and eastward to southern Quebec. It has been reared on dock (*Rumex* spp.) and dandelion (*Taraxacum officinale* Weber). The moth may be collected in July.

Agriopodes fallax (Herrich-Shaeffer)

Fig. 409

The CNC has material of this species from Georgian Bay, Ont., to Lac Mondor, Que. The larval food plant is arrowwood (*Viburnum* spp.). The adult may be collected in June and July.

Agriopodes teratophora (Herrich-Shaeffer)

Fig. 410

This species has been collected in southern and eastern Ontario and in western Quebec. The larva has been reared on mint (*Mentha* spp.). The moth may be collected in June and July.

Amphipyra pyramidoides Guenée

Fig. 411

This species is common across central and southern Ontario and in Quebec as far east as Lac Mondor. The larva feeds on a wide variety of broad-leaved trees. The adult may be collected in August and September.

Amphipyra tragopoginis (Linnaeus)

Fig. 412

This species is found from southern Ontario eastward to Forestville, Que. The larva feeds on hawthorn (*Crataegus* spp.), plantain (*Plantago* spp.), columbine (*Aquilegia* spp.), and geranium (*Geranium* spp.). The moth may be collected in July and August.

Amphipyra glabella (Morrison)

Fig. 420

This species has been collected from St. Thomas eastward to the Ottawa Valley, Ont., and Quebec City. The adult may be collected in late July and August. The larva feeds on poplar (*Populus* spp.).

Dipterygia scabriuscula (Linnaeus)

Fig. 413

This species occurs in Ontario from Hymers southward to Strathroy and eastward to Ottawa, and in western Quebec, at Meach Lake. The adult may be collected in June and July. The larva feeds on dock (*Rumex* spp.) and smartweed (*Polygonum* spp.).

Nedra ramosula (Guenée)

Fig. 423

This species is found from London, Ont., eastward to Lac Mondor, Que. It has been reared on St. John's-wort (*Hypericum perforatum* L.). The moth may be collected from June until September.

Andropolia contacta (Walker)

Fig. 421

The CNC has specimens of this species from Hymers and Sudbury, Ont. The moth may be collected in August.

Hyppa xylinoides (Guenée)

Fig. 424

This species is common across both Ontario and Quebec as far north as James Bay. The moth may be collected from June until September. The larva feeds on cranberry (*Vaccinium* spp.) and St. John's-wort (*Hypericum perforatum* L.).

Platysenta videns (Guenée)

Fig. 425

This species is represented in the CNC by material from southern and eastern Ontario, and also from Harrington Lake, in western Quebec. The larval food plants are aster (*Aster* spp.) and goldenrod (*Solidago* spp.). The moth may be collected from June until August.

Platysenta vecors (Guenée)

Fig. 426

This uncommon species has been collected from southern Ontario eastward to Ottawa and Montreal. The adult occurs from May until July.

Platysenta sutor (Guenée)

Fig. 422

A specimen in the CNC from Ancaster, in southern Ontario, was collected in September.

Elaphria versicolor (Guenée)

Fig. 465

This species is found throughout central and southern Ontario and Quebec. The adult may be collected in late June and July. The larva feeds on white spruce (*Picea glauca* (Moench) Voss), pine (*Pinus* spp.), and balsam fir (*Abies balsamea* (L.) Mill.).

Elaphria festivoides (Guenée)

Fig. 427

This species is common across Ontario and Quebec as far north as James Bay. The larva has been reared on Manitoba maple (*Acer negundo* L.). The moth may be collected in June.

Elaphria grata Hübner

Fig. 466

The CNC has only one specimen of this species; it was collected at Trenton, Ont. The larva feeds on violet (*Viola* spp.). The moth may be collected in October.

Elaphria georgei (Moore & Rawson)

Fig. 467

This species has been found at Laniel, in western Quebec, and at Ste. Foy, near Quebec City. The adult may be collected in June.

Platyperigea multifera (Walker)

Fig. 428

This species is found in Ontario from Hymers and London eastward to Ottawa, and in Quebec from Laniel to Montreal. The moth may be collected in August and early September.

Platyperigea meralis (Morrison)

Fig. 469

This species is very common in Western Canada. The CNC has specimens collected in eastern Ontario. The adult may be collected in August and September.

Crambodes talidiformis Guenée

Fig. 429

This species has been collected throughout southern and eastern Ontario from London to Ottawa. The larva has been reared on vervain (*Verbena* spp.). The adult may be collected from June until August.

Proxenus miranda (Grote)

Fig. 430

This species is found across both Ontario and Quebec as far north as the 50th parallel. The moths fly in June and July. The adult has been reared on dandelion (*Taraxacum officinale* Weber).

Proxenus mendosa McDunnough

Fig. 431

This western species has been found in the east only at Smoky Falls, in northern Ontario. The moth occurs in late June.

Galgula partita Guenée

Fig. 432

This species occurs from Black Sturgeon Lake across central and southern Ontario to western Quebec. The specimen in the photograph is a female. In this species, the males are usually lighter brown than the females. The moth may be collected in June and July.

Balsa malana (Fitch)

Fig. 433

This species is common in southern and eastern Ontario and western Quebec. The larva feeds on apple (*Pyrus* spp.). The moth may be collected in June and July.

Balsa tristrigella (Walker)

Fig. 440

The CNC has specimens of this species from southern and eastern Ontario and western Quebec. The larval food plant is hawthorn (*Crataegus* spp.). The adult may be collected in June.

Balsa labecula (Grote)

Fig. 435

The distribution of this species is similar to that of *B. tristrigella*. The moth may be collected from May until July.

Spodoptera ornithogalli (Guenée)

Fig. 439

In Ontario and Quebec, the species of this genus are considered migrants from the south. This species has been collected from southern Ontario to Ottawa. There are no specimens from Quebec in the CNC. The larva, commonly called the yellowstriped armyworm, feeds on clover (*Trifolium* spp.). The moth may be collected in June and September.

Spodoptera frugiperda (J. E. Smith)

Fig. 437

This species has been recorded as far north as Sault Ste. Marie, Ont., and Lac Mondor, Que. The larva is commonly called the fall armyworm. The moths are usually collected in September and early October.

Magusa orbifera (Walker)

Fig. 438

The CNC has material of this species from Chatham and Ottawa, Ont. It is considered a migrant from the south. The moth may be collected in the fall.

Enargia decolor (Walker)

Fig. 436

This species is common throughout the central regions of Ontario and Quebec from Manitoba to the Gaspé Peninsula. The larva feeds on eastern cottonwood (*Populus deltoides* Bartr.) and trembling apsen (*Populus tremuloides* Michx.). The moth may be collected in September.

Enargia infumata (Grote)

Fig. 434

This species has the same distribution as *E. decolor*. The two species are very similar, except for the presence of a small black spot in the lower end of the reniform of *E. infumata*. The larva feeds on trembling aspen (*Populus tremuloides* Michx.). The moth may be collected in July and August.

Cosmia calami (Harvey)

Fig. 441

This species is found in southern and eastern Ontario and in western Quebec. The larva feeds on red oak (*Quercus rubra* L.) and white oak (*Quercus alba* L.). The larva occasionally feeds on other caterpillars. The adult may be collected in July and August.

Amolita fessa Grote

Fig. 442

This uncommon species has been found in southern and eastern Ontario. There is no material from Quebec in the CNC. The adult occurs in July.

Arzama obliqua (Walker)

Fig. 443

This species has been collected throughout Ontario south of the 50th parallel and at Knowlton, Que. The larva, commonly called the cattail borer, bores into the crown of the plant and is completely solitary. The moth flies in June.

Bellura diffusa (Grote)

Fig. 444

This uncommon species occurs from Black Sturgeon Lake, Ont., to Lac Mondor, Que., and southward to Ottawa and Hamilton. The larva bores in the petioles of yellow pondlily (*Nuphar* spp.). The adult occurs in June and early July.

Achatodes zeae (Harris)

Fig. 445

This species is distributed from southern Ontario to western Quebec. The larva, commonly called the elder shoot borer, bores in the stems of elderberry (*Sambucus canadensis* L.). The adult may be collected in July and August.

Catabena lineolata Walker

Fig. 446

This species is found in southern and eastern Ontario and in western Quebec. The larva feeds on goldenrod (*Solidago* spp.). The moth may be collected in July.

Ogdoconta cinereola (Guenée)

Fig. 447

This species has been found in southern and eastern Ontario and at Lac Mondor, Que. The larva feeds on ragweed (*Ambrosia* spp.). The moth may be collected in June.

Subfamily Heliothidinae

The subfamily Heliothidinae contains about 150 species. Most of these are confined to western North America. One of the most characteristic features of the subfamily is that the larvae feed on the fruits and flowers of their hosts. The moths often visit the blossoms of the plants on which the larvae fed.

Eutricopis nexilis Morrison

Fig. 448

This species is found in central Ontario and western Quebec from Nipigon to Hull and Montreal, and southward to Gravenhurst. The larva feeds on the heads of pussytoes (*Antennaria* spp.). The moth may be collected in May.

Rhodoecia aurantiago (Guenée)

Fig. 470

This species is not common. There is material in the CNC from Grand Bend and Delhi, in southern Ontario. The larva feeds on seedpods of gerardia (*Gerardia* spp.). The moth occurs in August.

Pyrrhia umbra (Hufnagel)

Fig. 449

This species is found in southern and eastern Ontario and in western Quebec. The food plants are rose (*Rosa* spp.), sumac (*Rhus* spp.), and black walnut (*Juglans nigra* L.). The adult may be collected in June.

Pyrrhia exprimens (Walker)

Fig. 450

This species is prevalent across Ontario and Quebec as far north as James Bay. The larva feeds on a wide variety of plants. The moth may be collected in June and July.

Helicoverpa zea (Boddie)

Fig. 451

The larva of this species, commonly called the corn earworm, is an important pest in North America. The adult migrates into southern and eastern Ontario and western Quebec in July or August. Although the larva does not usually survive the winter in Canada, it can do a lot of damage to the ears of corn and the fruits of tomatoes during the late summer and fall.

Heliothis phloxiphaga Grote & Robinson

Fig. 471

This species has been collected in southern and eastern Ontario. There is no material from Quebec in the CNC. The larva feeds on aster (*Aster* spp.). The moth may be collected in June.

Heliothis borealis (Hampson)

Fig. 473

This species is more common in the west. The CNC has material from Cochrane and Timmins, in northern Ontario. The moth occurs in June. The larva feeds on larch (*Larix* spp.), white spruce (*Picea glauca* (Moench) Voss), and laurel (*Kalmia* spp.).

Heliothis virescens (Fabricius)

Fig. 474

The larva of this species, commonly called the tobacco budworm, is not considered a serious pest. The moth may be collected in July. It has been collected at Chatham, in southern Ontario. There is no material from Quebec in the CNC.

Heliothis paradoxa (Grote)

Fig. 475

This species may be a migrant from the south. The CNC has material from Chatham, in southern Ontario, that was collected in the late fall.

Schinia obscurata Strecker

Fig. 454

This species has been collected in southern and eastern Ontario. There are no specimens from Quebec in the CNC. The larva feeds on the flowers of fleabane (*Erigeron* spp.). The moth may be collected in June.

Schinia arcigera (Guenée)

Fig. 477

This species occurs across Ontario from Simcoe to Ottawa. The larva feeds on several species of aster (*Aster* spp.). The adult may be collected in September.

Schinia marginata (Haworth)

Fig. 478

This species occurs from Emo, in western Ontario, to Lac Mondor, Que. The larva feeds on ragweed (*Ambrosia* spp.). The adult may be collected in August.

Schinia thoreaui (Grote & Robinson)

Fig. 479

This species was collected from Chatham, in southern Ontario, in July. The larva feeds on the flowers of ragweed (*Ambrosia* spp.).

Schinia trifascia Hübner

Fig. 453

This species has been collected in southern and eastern Ontario. The larva feeds on Joe-Pye weed (*Eupatorium purpureum* L.). The adult may be collected from July until September.

Schinia florida (Guenée)

Fig. 452

This species occurs across Ontario and Quebec from Windsor eastward to

Lac Mondor. The larva feeds on the blossoms of yellow evening-primrose (*Oenothera biennis* L.). The moth may be collected in July and August.

Schinia meadi (Grote)

Fig. 480

This western species has been collected at Emo, in western Ontario. The moth occurs in July.

Schinia nundina (Drury)

Fig. 476

The CNC has several specimens that were collected at Chatham, in southern Ontario. The larva feeds on goldenrod (*Solidago* spp.). The moth may be collected during late July and August.

Subfamily Acontiinae

This subfamily contains approximately 160 species. Most of the moths rest with their wings folded in the shape of a very steep roof and some resemble bird droppings.

Cryphia pervertens Barnes & McDunnough

Fig. 455

This species has been collected in central and southern Ontario, from Kenora to Ottawa, and in Quebec, at Lac Mondor. The larva feeds on white elm (*Ulmus americana* L.) and bur oak (*Quercus macrocarpa* Michx.). The adult may be collected in July.

Cryphia villificans Barnes & McDunnough

Fig. 456

The only specimens in the CNC from Canada are from eastern Ontario. The larva feeds on white elm (*Ulmus americana* L.). The adult occurs in late June and July.

Protocryphia secta (Grote)

Fig. 457

This species has been collected in southernmost Ontario. The larva feeds on red oak (*Quercus rubra* L.) and white oak (*Quercus alba* L.). The adult may be collected in July.

Exyra rolandiana Grote

Fig. 458

This species is found only in sphagnum bogs where the larval host, the pitcherplant (*Sarracenia purpurea* L.), grows. There are specimens in the CNC from Thunder Bay, London, and several bogs in eastern Ontario. The adult may be collected in late June and early July.

Lithacodia bellicula Hübner

Fig. 459

This species is common in acid bogs throughout both Ontario and Quebec as far north as James Bay. The adult may be found in July and August.

Lithacodia albidula (Guenée)

Fig. 461

This species is common throughout Ontario and Quebec as far north as James Bay. The larva feeds on grasses (Gramineae). The adult may be collected during June and July.

Lithacodia muscosula (Guenée)

Fig. 460

This species has been collected in southern and eastern Ontario and in southern Quebec. The adult may be collected from June until August. The larva feeds on grasses (Gramineae).

Lithacodia synochitis (Grote & Robinson)

Fig. 462

This species is common across Ontario from London to Ottawa and in Quebec from Gracefield to Lac Mondor. The larva feeds on smartweed (*Polygonum* spp.). The moth may be collected during June and July.

Lithacodia concinnimacula (Guenée)

Fig. 463

The distribution of this species is similar to that of *L. synochitis*, but it does not appear to be as common. The adult may be collected from May until early July.

Lithacodia carneola (Guenée)

Fig. 464

This species is common in the southern half of both Ontario and Quebec as far north as Sudbury and the Gaspé Peninsula. The larva feeds on dock (*Rumex* spp.). The moth may be collected during July and August.

Neoerastria apicosa (Haworth)

Fig. 485

This species is represented in the CNC by material from southern and eastern Ontario and from western Quebec. The larva feeds on smartweed (*Polygonum* spp.). The moth may be collected during June and July.

Neoerastria caduca (Grote)

Fig. 472

The CNC has two specimens of this species, one is from Strathroy and the other is from Chaffey's Locks, Ont. The moth occurs in July; it is considered rare.

Capis curvata Grote

Fig. 486

This species occurs across both Ontario and Quebec from Smoky Falls to Lac Mondor. The adult may be collected during June and July.

Chamyris cerintha (Treitschke)

Fig. 487

This species has been collected in southern and eastern Ontario and in western Quebec. Rose (*Rosa* spp.), black cherry (*Prunus serotina* Ehrh.), and hawthorn (*Crataegus* spp.) are food plants of the larva. The moth may be collected in June and July.

Amyna bullula (Grote)

Fig. 468

This species has been collected at Beauport, Que., in August. This species is not common in collections.

Amyna octo (Guenée)

Fig. 481

This species is a migrant from the south that occasionally appears in Ontario in October. There is a specimen from Ottawa in the CNC. The larva feeds on goosefoot (*Chenopodium* spp.).

Tarachidia erastrioides (Guenée)

Fig. 488

This species has been collected in southern and eastern Ontario and in southern Quebec. The larva feeds on ragweed (*Ambrosia* spp.). The adult may be collected from June until August.

Tarachidia tortricina (Zeller)

Fig. 482

This primarily western species has been collected at Smoky Falls, in northern Ontario, during June.

Tarachidia candefacta (Hübner)

Fig. 489

This species is common from southern Ontario eastward to western Quebec. The larva has been reared on ragweed (*Ambrosia* spp.). The adult may be collected from June until August.

Acontia aprica (Hübner)

Fig. 483

This species is represented in the CNC by material from Chatham, Ont., collected in June. The larva feeds on hollyhock (*Althaea rosea* Cav.).

Acontia terminimaculata (Grote)

Fig. 490

This uncommon species has been collected in Ontario at Marmora and Trenton, and in the Eastern Townships of Quebec. The larva has been reared on basswood (*Tilia americana* L.). The moth occurs in July.

Subfamily Euteliinae

Eutelia pulcherrima (Grote)

Fig. 484

The only specimen of this species from Ontario was collected at Rondeau Park, in southern Ontario. The moth occurs in June. Poison sumac (*Rhus vernix* L.) is the food plant of the larva.

Marathyssa basalis Walker

Fig. 491

This species has been collected at a number of localities in eastern Ontario. There are no specimens from Quebec in the CNC. The larva feeds on poison-ivy (*Rhus radicans* L.). The moth may be collected in May.

Marathyssa inficita (Walker)

Fig. 492

This species has been collected in eastern Ontario and western Quebec. The larva feeds on staghorn sumac (*Rhus typhina* L.). The moth may be collected in June.

Paectes oculatrix (Guenée)

Fig. 493

This uncommon species has been collected in Ontario only at Port Colborne. The larva feeds on poison-ivy (*Rhus radicans* L.). The adult occurs in June.

Subfamily Sarrothripinae

Species in this subfamily are easily mistaken for moths of other families. The genus *Nycteola* is sometimes placed in a family of its own, the Nycteolidae.

Characoma nilotica (Rogenhofer)

Fig. 494

This uncommon species has been collected at various locations throughout the southern half of Ontario and Quebec from Black Sturgeon Lake to

Knowlton. The larva feeds on willow (*Salix* spp.) and azalea (*Rhododendron* spp.). The moth occurs in July and August.

Nycteola frigidana (Walker)

Fig. 495

This species has been collected from western and southern Ontario to western Quebec. The larva feeds on balsam poplar (*Populus balsamifera* L.) and willow (*Salix* spp.). The moth may be collected from June until August.

Nycteola cinereana Neumoegen & Dyar

This species can only be distinguished from *N. frigidana* by comparing the genitalia. The adult may be collected in central Ontario and western Quebec during July and August. The larva feeds on balsam poplar (*Populus balsamifera* L.). Not illustrated.

Baileya doubledayi (Guenée)

Fig. 496

This species is found from southern Ontario to the Gaspé Peninsula. The larva feeds on alder (*Alnus* spp.). The adult may be collected from June until August.

Baileya ophthalmica (Guenée)

Fig. 497

This species has been collected in southern and eastern Ontario and from western Quebec to Lac Mondor. The larva feeds on ironwood (*Ostrya virginiana* (Mill.) K. Koch). The adult may be collected in late May and June.
A similar species *Baileya australis* (Grote), with a straight rather than curved black line extending from the costa of the fore wing, has been collected in southern Ontario in July.

Baileya dormitans (Guenée)

Fig. 498

This species has been collected in southern and eastern Ontario and in Quebec from Hull to Quebec City. The adult may be collected in June and July. The larva feeds on ironwood (*Ostrya virginiana* (Mill.) K. Koch).

Subfamily Plusiinae

In North America the subfamily Plusiinae contains about 12 genera and 70 species. Many species have a prominent silver stigma in the center of the fore wing.

Caloplusia ignea similans McDunnough

Fig. 499

This species is represented in the CNC by material from Knob Lake, in northern Quebec. The moth may be collected in July.

Syngrapha parilis (Hübner)

Fig. 500

The CNC has material of this species from Payne Bay, Schefferville, and Port Harrison, in northern Quebec. The adult may be collected in late July and early August.

Syngrapha alticola (Walker)

Fig. 501

This species has been collected at Knob Lake, Que., in July.

Syngrapha microgamma montana (Packard)

Fig. 502

This species has been collected in Ontario at the Mer Bleue, near Ottawa, and in Quebec at Mt. Albert, in the Gaspé Peninsula. The adult may be collected in late June and July.

Syngrapha diasema (Boisduval)

Fig. 503

This species has been collected at Indian House Lake and Knob Lake, Que. The moth may be collected during late July and August.

Syngrapha rectangula (Kirby)

Fig. 504

Although this species occurs across the central regions of Ontario and

Quebec from the Manitoba border to the Gaspé Peninsula, it is usually uncommon. The larva feeds on eastern hemlock (*Tsuga canadensis* (L.) Carr.), spruce (*Picea* spp.), and balsam fir (*Abies balsamea* (L.) Mill.). The moth may be collected in June and July.

Syngrapha alias (Ottolengui)

Fig. 505

This species has been found in Ontario from Ogoki to Ottawa, and eastward to the Gaspé Peninsula, Que. The larva feeds on white spruce (*Picea glauca* (Moench) Voss) and black spruce (*Picea mariana* (Mill.) B.S.P.). The adult may be collected during July and August.

Syngrapha u-aureum (Aurivillius)

Fig. 506

This species has been collected at Port Harrison and Fort Chimo, in northern Quebec, during August. The larva feeds on blueberry (*Vaccinium* spp.).

Syngrapha interrogationis (Linnaeus)

Fig. 507

This European species has been collected in Quebec, only at Great Whale River. The larva feeds on blueberry (*Vaccinium* spp.). The adult occurs in August.

Syngrapha altera (Ottolengui)

Fig. 535

This species has been collected at Lake of the Woods and Larder Lake in Ontario and at Knob Lake in Quebec. The moth occurs in late July and August.

Syngrapha octoscripta (Grote)

Fig. 508

This species is common throughout both Ontario and Quebec as far north as James Bay. The moth may be collected during July and August.

Syngrapha surena (Grote)

Fig. 509

This uncommon species has been collected in Ontario at Smoky Falls, and in Quebec at Rimouski and Quebec City. The moth occurs in July and August.

Syngrapha epigaea (Grote)

Fig. 510

This species is found across the central regions of both Ontario and Quebec from Hymers to Lac Mondor and southward to Trenton. The moth may be collected during June and July. The larva feeds on blueberry (*Vaccinium* spp.).

Syngrapha selecta (Walker)

Fig. 511

This species occurs across Ontario and Quebec from Hymers and Ogoki eastward to Mistassini Post and the Gaspé Peninsula and southward to Lake Ontario. The larva feeds on spruce (*Picea* spp.), balsam fir (*Abies balsamea* (L.) Mill.), and pine (*Pinus* spp.). The adult may be collected in July.

Anagrapha falcifera (Kirby)

Fig. 512

This species is common in both Ontario and Quebec as far north as James Bay. The larva, commonly called the celery looper, occasionally damages celery and tobacco crops; it also feeds on dandelion (*Taraxacum officinale* Weber). The adult may be collected from June until September.

Trichoplusia ni (Hübner)

Fig. 513

This species is found throughout southern and eastern Ontario. The larva is commonly called the cabbage looper; it also feeds on a wide variety of garden crops. The moth may be collected from July until October.

Trichoplusia oxygramma (Geyer)

Fig. 536

This species is found in Ontario, only as a migrant from the south. The CNC has only one specimen from Ontario, collected at Delhi, in southern Ontario. The larva feeds on aster (*Aster* spp.) and goldenrod (*Solidago* spp.). The adult occurs in October.

Argyrogramma verruca (Fabricius)

Fig. 537

This is primarily a southern species, but it has been found as far north as Niagara Falls, Ont. The larva has been reared on arrowhead (*Sagittaria* spp.). The moth occurs in September.

Pseudoplusia oo (Cramer)

Fig. 514

This uncommon species has been collected at various locations from Hamilton to the Gaspé Peninsula. The larva is occasionally a greenhouse pest, especially on geranium. The adult occurs from July to October.

Chrysaspidia venusta (Walker)

Fig. 538

This species is often found in wet places; it has been collected in southern and eastern Ontario. There is no material from Quebec in the CNC. The moth may be collected from June until August.

Chrysaspidia putnami (Grote)

Fig. 515

This species occurs across Ontario and Quebec as far north as James Bay. The adult may be collected during July. The larva feeds on grasses (Gramineae).

Chrysaspidia contexta (Grote)

Fig. 516

This species has been collected in southern and eastern Ontario and in western Quebec. The larva feeds on grasses (Germineae). The moth may be collected in June and July.

Autographa biloba (Stephens)

Fig. 517

This species has been collected in southern and eastern Ontario and in western Quebec. The larva has been reared on dandelion (*Taraxacum officinale* Weber) and broad-leaved plantain (*Plantago major* L.). The moth may be collected during June and July.

Autographa precationis (Guenée)

Fig. 518

This common species occurs from southern Ontario to Lac Mondor, Que. The larva has been reared on dandelion (*Taraxacum officinale* Weber), broad-leaved plantain (*Plantago major* L.), and lamb's-quarters (*Chenopodium* spp.). The moth may be collected from July to October.

Autographa ampla (Walker)

Fig. 519

This species occurs from central and eastern Ontario to Forestville, Que. The larva feeds on alder (*Alnus* spp.), cherry (*Prunus* spp.), and willow (*Salix* spp.). The moth may be collected in July and early August.

Autographa sansoni Dod

Fig. 520

This western species has been collected only once in the east, at Alcove, in western Quebec, in June.

Autographa rubida Ottolengui

Fig. 521

This species has been collected from Smoky Falls to Ottawa, Ont., and Knowlton, Que. The adult may be collected in late June and July.

Autographa bimaculata (Stephens)

Fig. 522

This species occurs throughout both Ontario and Quebec as far north as James Bay. The moth may be collected in late July and early August.

Autographa mappa (Grote & Robinson)

Fig. 523

This species has been collected from Smoky Falls and Larder Lake southward to Lake Ontario and eastward to Lac Mondor and Forestville, Que. The larva feeds on stinging nettle (*Urtica dioica* L.). The adult may be collected in June and July.

Autographa pseudogamma (Grote)

Fig. 524

This species occurs across the central regions of both Ontario and Quebec from Black Sturgeon Lake to the Gaspé Peninsula. The moth may be collected during June and July.

Autographa flagellum (Walker)

Fig. 525

This species occurs from western Ontario to Smoky Falls and southward to Hamilton and Ottawa, and to Knowlton, Que. The moth may be collected in June and July.

Chrysanympha formosa (Grote)

Fig. 526

This uncommon species has been collected from Black Sturgeon Lake, Ont., to Lac Mondor, Que., and southward to Ottawa. The larva feeds on blueberry (*Vaccinium* spp.). The moth occurs in June and July.

Eosphoropteryx thyatyroides (Guenée)

Fig. 527

This species has been collected in eastern Ontario and western Quebec. The larva feeds on meadow-rue (*Thalictrum* spp.). The moth may be collected in August.

Pseudeva purpurigera (Walker)

Fig. 528

This species has been collected from western Ontario to Lac Mondor, Que., and southward throughout southern Quebec and Ontario. The larva feeds on meadow-rue (*Thalictrum* spp.). The moth may be collected in June and July.

Plusia balluca (Geyer)

Fig. 529

This species has been collected from western Ontario to Lac Mondor, Que., and southward to Trenton, Ont. The larva feeds on raspberry (*Rubus* spp.). The moth may be collected during July.

Plusia aereoides Grote

Fig. 530

This species occurs across the central and southern part of Ontario and Quebec, from western Ontario to Lac Mondor, Que. The moth may be collected in July. The larva feeds on aster (*Aster* spp.).

Allagrapha aerea (Hübner)

Fig. 531

This species has been collected from southern Ontario eastward to Lac Mondor, Que. The moth may be collected during August and September. It has been reared on dandelion (*Taraxacum officinale* Weber).

Abrostola urentis Guenée

Fig. 532

This species has been collected from Smoky Falls, Ont., southward to western Quebec and southern Ontario. The larva has been reared on nettle (*Urtica* spp.). The adult may be collected in June and July.

Subfamily Catocalinae

The subfamily Catocalinae is made up of about 70 genera and 300 species. Many species in the genus *Catocala* have brightly colored hind wings.

The black witch (*Erebus odora* (L.)) and the owl moth (*Thysania zenobia* (Cram.)), the two largest noctuid moths found in North America, are in this subfamily. They occasionally migrate into Ontario and Quebec from the tropics in late autumn.

The larvae of the Catocalinae feed mainly on trees and shrubs.

Catocala innubens Guenée

Figs. 533, 613

This species is represented in the CNC by material from Simcoe and Oshawa, Ont. The larva feeds on honey-locust (*Gleditsia triacanthos* L.). The adult may be collected in August.

Catocala piatrix Grote

Fig. 595

This species has been collected throughout southern Ontario and occasionally in eastern Ontario. The larva feeds on hickory (*Carya* spp.), black walnut (*Juglans nigra* L.), and butternut (*Juglans cinerea* L.). The moth may be collected in August.

Catocala epione (Drury)

Fig. 534

The only specimens of this species from Canada were collected in the vicinity of Kingston, Ont. The larva feeds on shagbark hickory (*Carya ovata* (Mill.) K. Koch). The moth occurs in late July and August.

Catocala antinympha (Hübner)

Fig. 572

This species occurs in central and eastern Ontario and western Quebec where its food plant sweet-fern (*Myrica asplenifolia* L.) is found. The moth may be collected in July and early August.

Catocala coelebs Grote

Fig. 573

This species has been collected in Ontario at Toronto and Smith Falls. The moth may be collected in August. The larva feeds on sweet gale (*Myrica gale* L.).

Catocala habilis Grote

Fig. 574

This species is found throughout southern and southeastern Ontario. The moth may be collected during August and September. The larva feeds on hickory (*Carya* spp.) and walnut (*Juglans* spp.).

Catocala serena Edwards

Fig. 575

The only specimen of this rare species from Canada in the CNC is labeled "eastern Ontario." The moth was collected in August.

Catocala obscura Strecker

Fig. 590

This species has been collected in southern and eastern Ontario as far north as Ottawa. This species is most easily distinguished from *Catocala residua* by the white fringe on the hind wing. The moth may be collected during August.

Catocala residua Grote

Fig. 591

This species has been collected at Toronto. The moth may be collected in August. The larva feeds on hickory (*Carya* spp.).

Catocala retecta Grote

Fig. 593

This species has been collected in southern and eastern Ontario as far east as Ottawa. The moth may be collected during August and September. The larva feeds on hickory (*Carya* spp.).

Catocala insolabilis Guenée

Fig. 592

There are specimens in the CNC labeled "eastern Ontario" and "Toronto" that were collected in July. The larva feeds on hickory (*Carya* spp.).

Catocala vidua (J. E. Smith)

Fig. 594

This species has been collected in southern Ontario as far east as Toronto. The larva feeds on hickory (*Carya* spp.) and walnut (*Juglans* spp.). The adult may be collected in September.

Catocala palaeogama Guenée

Fig. 596

This species has been collected in southern and eastern Ontario as far east as Brockville. The moth may be collected in August. The larva feeds on hickory (*Carya* spp.) and walnut (*Juglans* spp.).

Catocala subnata Grote

Fig. 597

This species occurs in southern and eastern Ontario and in western Quebec. The moth may be collected from July to September.

Catocala neogama (J. E. Smith)

Fig. 598

This species has been collected in southern and eastern Ontario as far east as Chaffey's Locks. The moth may be collected in August and September. The larva feeds on hickory (*Carya* spp.) and walnut (*Juglans* spp.).

Catocala ilia (Cramer)

Figs. 605, 606

This species is fairly common. It is found from southern Ontario to Lac Mondor, Que. The moth may be collected during July and August. The larva feeds on oak (*Quercus* spp.).

Catocala cerogama Guenée

Fig. 599

This species has been collected from southern Ontario to Lac Mondor, Que. The larva feeds on poplar (*Populus* spp.) and basswood (*Tilia americana* L.). The moth may be collected in August and early September.

Catocala relicta Walker

Figs. 600, 601

This species is common across Ontario and Quebec as far north as James Bay. The moth may be collected in August and September. The larva feeds on trembling aspen (*Populus tremuloides* Michx.) and willow (*Salix* spp.).

Catocala unijuga Walker

Fig. 611

This species is common across Quebec and Ontario as far north as Ogoki, Ont. The moth may be collected in August and September. The larva feeds on poplar (*Populus* spp.) and willow (*Salix* spp.).

Catocala parta Guenée

Fig. 607

This species is common in southern and eastern Ontario. There are no specimens from Quebec in the CNC. The larva feeds on poplar (*Populus* spp.) and willow (*Salix* spp.). The adult may be collected from late July to late August.

Catocala briseis Edwards

Figs. 608, 609

This species is common across Ontario and Quebec as far north as Ogoki, Ont. The adult may be collected in late July and August. The larva feeds on poplar (*Populus* spp.) and willow (*Salix* spp.).

Catocala semirelicta Grote

Fig. 612

This species has been collected from Hymers, Ont., to Lake St. John and southward to south central Quebec and Toronto. The adult may be collected in August and September. The larva feeds on poplar (*Populus* spp.).

Catocala meskei Grote

Fig. 610

This species has been collected from southern Ontario eastward to Quebec City. The moth may be collected in late July and early August.

Catocala cara Guenée

Fig. 604

This species has been collected in southern Ontario as far east as Hamilton. The moth may be collected in August and September. The larva feeds on willow (*Salix* spp.).

Catocala concumbens Walker

Fig. 584

This species is common in both Ontario and Quebec from southern Ontario to Lac Mondor. The larva feeds on poplar (*Populus* spp.) and willow (*Salix* spp.). The adult may be collected in August.

Catocala amatrix (Hübner)

Figs. 602, 603

This species occurs in southern and eastern Ontario. The moth may be collected from late August until early October. The larva feeds on poplar (*Populus* spp.).

Catocala sordida Grote

Fig. 582

This species has been collected from central and eastern Ontario to Forestville, Que. The larva feeds on blueberry (*Vaccinium* spp.). The moth may be collected in July.

Catocala coccinata Grote

Fig. 579

This species has been collected in southern and eastern Ontario. The moth may be collected in July. The larva feeds on oak (*Quercus* spp.).

Catocala ultronia (Hübner)

Fig. 578

This species is common throughout the southern half of both Ontario and Quebec from Hymers to Forestville. The moth may be collected from June until August. The larva feeds on cherry and plum (*Prunus* spp.).

Catocala crataegi Saunders

Fig. 577

This species is fairly common in southern and eastern Ontario. The moth may be collected in July. The larva feeds on hawthorn (*Crataegus* spp.).

Catocala mira Grote

Fig. 576

This species has been collected in southern and eastern Ontario. The moth may be collected in July. The larva feeds on hawthorn (*Crataegus* spp.).

Catocala grynea (Cramer)

Fig. 586

This species is common in southern Ontario as far east as Hamilton. The moth may be collected in July. The larva feeds on apple (*Pyrus* spp.), plum (*Prunus* spp.), and hawthorn (*Crataegus* spp.).

Catocala praeclara Grote & Robinson

Fig. 583

This uncommon species has been collected at widely scattered localities from southern Ontario to Lac Mondor, Que. The larva feeds on hawthorn (*Crataegus* spp.). The moth occurs during July and August.

Catocala blandula Hulst

Fig. 581

This species occurs throughout the southern half of Ontario and Quebec from Hymers, Ont., to Forestville, Que. The larva feeds on hawthorn (*Crataegus* spp.). The moth may be collected in July and August.

Catocala clintonii Grote

Fig. 580

The CNC has representatives of this species from Trenton, Chaffey's Locks, and Westport, in eastern Ontario. The moth may be collected in late June and July. The larva feeds on wild plum (*Prunus americana* Marsh.).

Catocala similis Edwards

Fig. 588

There are specimens of this species in the CNC from eastern Ontario and from Norway Bay, in western Quebec. The larva feeds on oak (*Quercus* spp.). The adult may be collected in July.

Catocala micronympha Guenée

Fig. 587

Although this species is widespread in eastern United States, the only specimen from Ontario is labeled "eastern Ontario" and it was collected in July. The larva feeds on oak (*Quercus* spp.).

Catocala amica (Hübner)

Fig. 589

This species has been collected in southern and southeastern Ontario. The moth may be collected in July. The larva feeds on oak (*Quercus* spp.).

Euparthenos nubilis (Hübner)

Fig. 585

This species is fairly common in southern and eastern Ontario, where its food plant black-locust (*Robinia pseudoacacia* L.) grows. The moth may be collected in July and August.

Parallelia bistriaris Hübner

Fig. 539

This species is found from southern Ontario to Lac Mondor, Que. It has been reared on red maple (*Acer rubrum* L.). The moth may be collected in June.

Euclidia cuspidea (Hübner)

Fig. 540

This species is prevalent throughout both Ontario and Quebec as far north as James Bay. The moth may be collected in June. The larva feeds on clover (*Trifolium* spp.).

Caenurgina crassiuscula (Haworth)

Fig. 541

This species is abundant throughout Ontario and Quebec as far north as James Bay. The moth may be collected from May until September. The larva, commonly called the clover looper, feeds on grasses (Gramineae).

Caenurgina erechtea (Cramer)

Fig. 542

This species is similar to *C. crassiuscula,* and is difficult to distinguish from it except by genitalic characters. It has been collected from southern Ontario to Lac Mondor, Que. The adult may be collected from early June until September. The larva, commonly called the forage looper, feeds on clover (*Trifolium* spp.).

Mocis latipes (Guenée)

Fig. 543

Adults of this species are found occasionally in southern Ontario in October. Specimens have been collected at Toronto and Ottawa. In the south, the larva is occasionally a pest in gardens on rice, turnips, broad beans, and corn.

Argyrostrotis anilis (Drury)

Fig. 544

This uncommon species has been collected in southern and eastern Ontario and in western Quebec. The adult occurs in June and July.

Zale lunata (Drury)

Fig. 545

This species is common in southern Ontario and Quebec as far north as Hymers and Montreal. The larva feeds on most deciduous trees including cherry (*Prunus* spp.), maple (*Acer* spp.), and willow (*Salix* spp.). The moth may be collected from late August to early October.

Zale unilineata (Grote)

Fig. 546

This species is found in Ontario from Hymers to Ottawa and in Quebec at Lac Mondor. The moth may be collected in May. The larva has been reared on black-locust (*Robinia pseudoacacia* L.).

Zale galbanata (Morrison)

Fig. 547

This species has been found in southern and eastern Ontario. There are no specimens from Quebec in the CNC. The larva feeds on Manitoba maple (*Acer negundo* L.). The moth may be collected in June and July.

Zale aeruginosa (Guenée)

Fig. 548

This species has been collected from Black Sturgeon Lake, Ont., across central and eastern Ontario to western Quebec. The moth may be collected in late May and June.

Zale undularis (Drury)

Fig. 549

This species has been collected in southern and eastern Ontario. The adult may be collected in June. The larva feeds on black-locust (*Robinia pseudoacacia* L.).

Zale minerea (Guenée)

Fig. 550

This species is common throughout the southern half of Ontario and Quebec from Hymers, Ont., to Forestville, Que. The adult may be collected in May and early June. The larva feeds on birch (*Betula* spp.), beech (*Fagus* spp.), maple (*Acer* spp.), and poplar (*Populus* spp.).

Zale lunifera (Hübner)

Fig. 551

This species has been collected from central and eastern Ontario to Lac Mondor, Que. The adult may be collected in May. The larva feeds on black cherry (*Prunus serotina* Ehrh.).

Zale submediana McDunnough

Fig. 552

This species is found across the central portion of Ontario and Quebec from western Ontario to western Quebec. The adult may be collected in late April and May. The larva feeds on jack pine (*Pinus banksiana* Lamb.).

Zale duplicata (Bethune)

Fig. 553

This species has been collected from Hymers, Ont., to western Quebec and southward to London, Ont. The larva has been reared on eastern white pine (*Pinus strobus* L.), jack pine (*Pinus banksiana* Lamb.), and tamarack (*Larix laricina* (Du Roi) K. Koch). The moth may be collected in May and June.

Zale helata (Smith)

Fig. 554

This species occurs from western Ontario to western Quebec and southward to southern Ontario. The larva feeds on eastern white pine (*Pinus strobus* L.) and jack pine (*Pinus banksiana* Lamb.). The adult may be collected in late May and June.

Zale horrida Hübner

Fig. 555

This species is found in southern and eastern Ontario and in western Quebec. The moth may be collected in late May and June. The larva has been reared on nannyberry (*Viburnum lentago* L.).

Erebus odora (Linnaeus)

Fig. 562

This tropical species occasionally flies north in the fall. It is commonly called the black witch. Specimens have been collected at Toronto, Kingston, and at Meach Lake and in the Gaspé Peninsula, Que.

Thysania zenobia (Cramer)

Fig. 563

This tropical species is much rarer than *E. odora*. The moth occasionally flies north in August and September. Specimens have been collected at Point Pelee and Chatham, in southern Ontario.

Panopoda rufimargo (Hübner)

Fig. 556

This species has been collected from southern Ontario to Lac Mondor, Que. The larva feeds on beech (*Fagus grandifolia* Ehrh.) and oak (*Quercus* spp.). The moth occurs in July.

Panopoda carneicosta Guenée

Fig. 557

The CNC has material of this species from southern and eastern Ontario. There are no specimens from Quebec in the CNC. The moth may be collected during July and August. The larva feeds on oak (*Quercus* spp.), hickory (*Carya* spp.), and willow (*Salix* spp.).

Cissusa spadix (Cramer)

Fig. 558

This species is an occasional migrant from the south. Specimens have been collected at Toronto and Ottawa in April.

Phoberia atomaris Hübner

Fig. 559

The CNC has material of this species from eastern Ontario that was collected in April and May. The larva feeds on oak (*Quercus* spp.).

Synedoida grandirena (Haworth)

Fig. 560

This species has been collected in southern Ontario and at Hemingford, in the Eastern Townships of Quebec. The larva feeds on witch-hazel (*Hamamelis virginiana* L.). The moth may be collected in June and July.

Synedoida adumbrata alleni (Grote)

Fig. 561

This species has been collected at Sudbury and Ottawa, Ont., and from Laniel and Norway Bay to Forestville, Que. The adult may be collected in June.

Calpe canadensis Bethune

Fig. 568

This species has been collected from southern and central Ontario eastward to Lac Mondor, Que. The larva feeds on meadow-rue (*Thalictrum* spp.). The moth may be collected in late July and August.

Anticarsia gemmatalis Hübner

Fig. 564

This is a common tropical species that moves northward in October, sometimes in very large numbers. The CNC has specimens from southern and eastern Ontario. The larva, commonly called the velvetbean caterpillar, injures velvet bean (*Stizolobium* spp.) in the south.

Strenoloma lunilinea (Grote)

Fig. 566

This species is not common in the northern part of its range. The CNC has specimens from Normandale, London, and Ancaster, in southern Ontario. The larva feeds on honey-locust (*Gleditsia triacanthos* L.). The moth occurs in July.

Plusiodonta compressipalpis Guenée

Fig. 565

This species is distributed across southern and eastern Ontario. The larva feeds on moonseed (*Menispermum canadense* L.). The adult may be collected from June until August.

Hypocala andremona (Cramer)

Fig. 570

This is a tropical species that occasionally migrates as far north as southern Ontario. There is a specimen in the CNC from London.

Scoliopteryx libatrix (Linnaeus)

Fig. 571

This species is common throughout both Ontario and Quebec as far north as James Bay. The moth lives from July until the following May, overwintering as an adult. The larva feeds on willow (*Salix* spp.) and poplar (*Populus* spp.).

Alabama argillacea (Hübner)

Fig. 567

In Ontario, this species is a migrant from the south. It breeds each summer in the cotton belt and often flies north in September and October. It has been collected in southern and eastern Ontario. The larva is commonly called the cotton leafworm.

Anomis erosa Hübner

Fig. 569

The adults of this southern species migrate northward in September and October. There are specimens in the CNC from Delhi, Ont., and St. Jean, Que.

Figs. 1–18. 1, *Alypia octomaculata* (Fabricius), ♀; 2, *A. octomaculata* (Fabricius), ♂; 3, *A. langtoni* Couper, ♀; 4, *A. langtoni* Couper, ♂; 5, *Androloma mac-cullochi* (Kirby), ♀; 6, *Euthisanotia grata* (Fabricius), ♀; 7, *E. unio* Hübner, ♂; 8, *Colocasia flavicornis* (Smith), ♂; 9, *C. propinquilinea* (Grote), ♂; 10, *Panthea acronyctoides* (Walker), ♀; 11, *P. pallescens* McDunnough, ♀; 12, *Charadra deridens* (Guenée), ♂; 13, *Acronicta spinigera* Guenée, ♀; 14, *Chersotis juncta* (Grote), ♂; 15, *Diarsia pseudorosaria freemani* Hardwick, ♂; 16, *Euxoa ridingsiana* (Grote), ♀; 17, *E. sinelinea* Hardwick, ♀; 18, *E. drewseni* (Staudinger), ♀.

Figs. 19–35. 19, *Raphia frater* Grote, ♂; 20, *Acronicta lepusculina* Guenée, ♂; 21, *A. innotata* Guenée, ♂; 22, *A. leporina* (Linnaeus), ♂; 23, *A. rubricoma* Guenée, ♀; 24, *A. tritona* (Hübner), ♂; 25, *A. americana* Harris, ♀; 26, *A. dactylina* (Grote), ♀; 27, *A. radcliffei* (Harvey), ♂; 28, *A. grisea* Walker, ♂; 29, *A. albarufa* (Grote), ♀; 30, *A. connecta* Grote, ♂; 31, *A. funeralis* Grote & Robinson, ♂; 32, *A. quadrata* (Grote), ♂; 33, *A. vinnula* (Grote), ♂; 34, *A. superans* Guenée, ♀; 35, *A. laetifica* Smith, ♂.

Figs. 36–53. *Acronicta* spp. 36, *A. furcifera* Guenée, ♂; 37, *A. modica* Walker, ♀; 38, *A. hasta* Guenée, ♀; 39, *A. interrupta* Guenée, ♂; 40, *A. fragilis* (Guenée), ♂; 41, *A. pruni* Harris, ♀; 42, *A. morula* Grote & Robinson, ♂; 43, *A. ovata* Grote, ♀; 44, *A. haesitata* (Grote), ♀; 45, *A. afflicta* Grote, ♂; 46, *A. inclara* Smith, ♀; 47, *A. tristis* Smith, ♂; 48, *A. hamamelis* Guenée, ♂; 49, *A. increta* Morrison, ♀; 50, *A. subochrea* Grote, ♂; 51, *A. retardata* (Walker), ♀; 52, *A. clarescens* Guenée, ♀; 53, *A. impleta* Walker, ♀.

Figs. 54–71. 54, *Acronicta sperata* Grote, ♂; 55, *A. noctivaga* Grote, ♂; 56, *A. impressa* Walker, ♀; 57, *A. oblinita* (J. E. Smith), ♂; 58, *A. lithospila* Grote, ♂; 59, *Harrisimemna trisignata* (Walker), ♂; 60, *Simyra henrici* (Grote), ♂; 61, *Acronicta lanceolaria* (Grote), ♀; 62, *Euxoa dissona* (Möschler), ♀; 63, *E. servita* (Smith), ♂; 64, *E. redimicula* (Morrison), ♂; 65, *E. albipennis* (Grote), ♂; 66, *E. declarata* (Walker), ♀; 67, *E. divergens* (Walker), ♀; 68, *E. obeliscoides* (Guenée), ♀; 69, *E. tessellata* (Harris), ♀; 70, *E. bostoniensis* (Grote), ♀; 71, *E. ontario* (Smith), ♀.

Figs. 72–89. 72, *Euxoa fumalis* (Grote), ♂; 73, *E. scholastica* McDunnough, ♂; 74, *E. messoria* (Harris), ♀; 75, *E. mimallonis* (Grote), ♀; 76, *E. velleripennis* (Grote), ♂; 77, *E. detersa* (Walker), ♀; 78, *E. quebecensis* (Smith), ♂; 79, *E. manitobana* McDunnough, ♂; 80, *E. aurulenta* (Smith), ♂; 81, *E. churchillensis* (McDunnough), ♀; 82, *E. chimoensis* Hardwick, ♂; 83, *E. pleuritica* (Grote), ♀; 84, *E. ochrogaster* (Guenée), ♂; 85, *E. ochrogaster* (Guenée), ♀; 86, *E. campestris* (Grote), ♀; 87, *Pachnobia wockei* (Möschler), ♂; 88, *Amathes xanthographa* (Fabricius), ♂; 89, *Anomogyna laetabilis* (Zetterstedt), ♂.

Figs. 90–107. 90, *Euxoa perpolita* (Morrison), ♂; 91, *E. scandens* (Riley), ♂; 92, *Agrotis vetusta* Walker, ♂; 93, *A. mollis* Walker, ♀; 94, *A. patula* Walker, ♂; 95, *A. gladiaria* Morrison, ♂; 96, *A. venerabilis* Walker, ♂; 97, *A. volubilis* Harvey, ♂; 98, *A. obliqua* (Smith), ♂; 99, *A. ipsilon* (Hufnagel), ♂; 100, *Feltia jaculifera* Guenée, ♂; 101, *F. geniculata* (Grote & Robinson), ♀; 102, *F. herilis* (Grote), ♂; 103, *F. subgothica* (Haworth), ♂; 104, *Actebia fennica* (Tauscher), ♀; 105, *Spaelotis clandestina* (Harris), ♀; 106, *Choephora fungorum* Grote & Robinson, ♂; 107, *Ochropleura plecta* (Linnaeus), ♂.

Figs. 108–125. 108, *Eurois astricta* Morrison, ♂; 109, *Metalepsis salicarum* (Walker), ♂; 110, *Cerastis tenebrifera* (Walker), ♀; 111, *Eurois occulta* (Linnaeus), ♀; 112, *Euagrotis illapsa* (Walker), ♂; 113, *Hemipachnobia monochromatea* (Morrison), ♂; 114, *Peridroma saucia* (Hübner), ♂; 115, *Metalepsis fishii* (Grote), ♂; 116, *Euagrotis forbesi* Franclemont, ♀; 117, *Paradiarsia littoralis* (Packard), ♂; 118, *Graphiphora haruspica* (Grote), ♀; 119, *Diarsia rubifera* (Grote), ♂; 120, *Heptagrotis phyllophora* (Grote), ♀; 121, *Rhyacia quadrangula* (Zetterstedt), ♀; 122, *Diarsia dislocata* (Smith), ♂; 123, *D. jucunda* (Walker), ♂; 124, *Amathes c-nigrum* (Linnaeus), ♀; 125, *A. smithii* (Snellen), ♀.

Figs. 126–143. 126, *Amathes badinodis* (Grote), ♂; 127, *A. normaniana* (Grote), ♂; 128, *A. collaris* (Grote & Robinson), ♀; 129, *A. bicarnea* (Guenée), ♂; 130, *A. tenuicula* (Morrison), ♂; 131, *A. opacifrons* (Grote), ♂; 132, *Pachnobia tecta* (Hübner), ♂; 133, *P. scropulana* (Morrison), ♂; 134, *P. okakensis* (Packard), ♀; 135, *Anomogyna atrata* (Morrison), ♂; 136, *A. fabulosa* Ferguson, ♂; 137, *A. speciosa* (Hübner), ♂; 138, *A. perquiritata* (Morrison), ♂; 139, *A. homogena* McDunnough, ♂; 140, *A. imperita* (Hübner), ♂; 141, *A. elimata* (Guenée), ♂; 142, *A. dilucida* (Morrison), ♂; 143, *A. youngii* (Smith), ♂.

Figs. 144–161.   144, *Aplectoides condita* (Guenée), ♂ ; 145, *Anaplectoides pressus* (Grote), ♂ ; 146, *Cryptocala acadiensis* (Bethune), ♂ ; 147, *Protolampra rufipectus* (Morrison), ♀ ; 148, *P. brunneicollis* (Grote), ♀ ; 149, *Anaplectoides prasina* (Schiffermüller), ♂ ; 150, *Eueretagrotis sigmoides* (Guenée), ♂ ; 151, *E. perattenta* (Grote), ♂ ; 152, *E. attenta* (Grote), ♀ ; 153, *E. perattenta* (Grote), ♀ ; 154, *Abagrotis alternata* (Grote), ♂ ; 155, *Polia nimbosa* (Guenée), ♂ ; 156, *Rhynchagrotis anchocelioides* (Guenée), ♀ ; 157, *Ufeus satyricus* Grote, ♂ ; 158, *Scotogramma trifolii* (Rottenburg), ♂ ; 159, *Tricholea artesta* (Smith), ♂ ; 160, *Mamestra curialis* (Smith), ♀ ; 161, *Rhynchagrotis cupida* (Grote), ♂.

Figs. 162–179. 162, *Polia segregata* (Smith), ♂; 163, *Lacinipolia implicata* McDunnough, ♂; 164, *Polia ingravis* (Smith), ♂; 165, *P. secedens* (Walker), ♂; 166, *P. carbonifera* (Hampson), ♂; 167, *Lasionycta albinuda* (Smith), ♂; 168, *Astrapetis sutrina* (Grote), ♂; 169, *Stretchia plusiaeformis* Edwards, ♂; 170, *Leucania linita* Guenée, ♀; 171, *Polia leomegra* (Smith), ♂; 172, *Morrisonia distincta* (Hübner), ♀; 173, *Polia atlantica* (Grote), ♂; 174, *P. imbrifera* (Guenée), ♂; 175, *P. grandis* (Boisduval), ♂; 176, *P. subjuncta* (Grote & Robinson), ♂; 177, *P. purpurissata* (Grote), ♂; 178, *P. latex* (Guenée), ♀; 179, *P. nevadae* (Grote), ♂.

Figs. 180–197. 180, *Polia radix* (Walker), ♀; 181, *P. legitima* (Grote), ♂; 182, *P. tacoma* (Strecker), ♀; 183, *P. rugosa* (Morrison), ♂; 184, *P. lilacina* (Harvey), ♀; 185, *P. adjuncta* (Boisduval), ♀; 186, *P. assimilis* (Morrison), ♂; 187, *P. pulverulenta* (Smith), ♀; 188, *P. cristifera* (Walker), ♂; 189, *P. lutra* (Guenée), ♂; 190, *P. detracta* (Walker), ♂; 191, *P. goodelli* (Grote), ♂; 192, *P. obscura* (Smith), ♂; 193, *Lacinipolia meditata* (Grote), ♀; 194, *L. lustralis* (Grote), ♂; 195, *L. anguina* (Grote), ♂; 196, *L. vicina* (Grote), ♀; 197, *L. renigera* (Stephens), ♂.

Figs. 198–215. 198, *Lacinipolia lorea* (Guenée), ♂; 199, *L. olivacea* (Morrison), ♂; 200, *Lasionycta subdita* (Möschler), ♀; 201, *Lasiestra phoca* (Möschler), ♂; 202, *L. uniformis* (Smith), ♀; 203, *Anarta cordigera* (Thunberg), ♀; 204, *A. melanopa* (Thunberg), ♂; 205, *A. richardsoni* (Curtis), ♀; 206, *Sideridis rosea* (Harvey), ♂; 207, *S. congermana* (Morrison), ♀; 208, *S. maryx* (Guenée), ♀; 209, *Anepia capsularis* (Guenée), ♀; 210, *Tricholita signata* (Walker), ♂; 211, *Ulolonche modesta* (Morrison), ♀; 212, *U. culea* (Guenée), ♀; 213, *Protorthodes oviduca* (Guenée), ♂; 214, *Homorthodes furfurata* (Grote), ♂; 215, *Pseudorthodes vecors* (Guenée), ♀.

Figs. 216–233. 216, *Orthodes crenulata* (Butler), ♀; 217, *O. cynica* Guenée, ♂; 218, *Anhimella contrahens* (Walker), ♂; 219, *Nephelodes minians* Guenée, ♂; 220, *Morrisonia evicta* (Grote), ♀; 221, *M. confusa* (Hübner), ♀; 222, *Xylomyges dolosa* Grote, ♂; 223, *Orthosia rubescens* (Walker), ♂; 224, *O. revicta* (Morrison), ♂; 225, *O. hibisci* (Guenée), ♂; 226, *Crocigrapha normani* (Grote), ♀; 227, *Ceramica picta* (Harris), ♂; 228, *Faronta diffusa* (Walker), ♂; 229, *Leucania pseudargyria* Guenée, ♂; 230, *L. ursula* Forbes, ♀; 231, *L. inermis* Forbes, ♂; 232, *L. commoides* Guenée, ♂; 233, *L. phragmatidicola* Guenée, ♀.

Figs. 234–251. 234, *Cucullia omissa* Dod, ♂; 235, *Leucania insueta* Guenée, ♂; 236, *Pseudaletia unipuncta* (Haworth), ♂; 237, *Aletia oxygala* (Grote), ♂; 238, *Cucullia speyeri* Lintner, ♂; 239, *C. intermedia* Speyer, ♂; 240, *C. florea* Guenée, ♂; 241, *Leucania multilinea* Walker, ♂; 242, *Cucullia postera* Guenée, ♂; 243, *C. asteroides* Guenée, ♂; 244, *C. convexipennis* Grote & Robinson, ♂; 245, *Oncocnemis saundersiana* Grote, ♀; 246, *O. piffardi* (Walker), ♀; 247, *O. riparia* Morrison, ♀; 248, *Homohadena badistriga* (Grote), ♂; 249, *Adita chionanthi* (J. E. Smith), ♀; 250, *Apharetra purpurea* McDunnough, ♂; 251, *Sympistis funesta* (Paykull), ♀.

Figs. 252–269. 252, *Homohadena infixa* (Walker), ♀; 253, *Sympistis labradoris* (Staudinger), ♂; 254, *S. melaleuca* (Thunberg), ♂; 255, *S. lapponica* (Thunberg), ♂; 256, *Brachionycha borealis* (Smith), ♂; 257, *Sympistis kolthoffi* (Aurivillius), ♂; 258, *Eutolype rolandi* Grote, ♂; 259, *Copipanolis styracis* (Guenée), ♂; 260, *Hillia iris* (Zetterstedt), ♂; 261, *Feralia jocosa* (Guenée), ♂; 262, *F. major* Smith, ♂; 263, *F. comstocki* Grote, ♂; 264, *Copivaleria grotei* (Morrison), ♀; 265, *Psaphida thaxteriana* (Grote), ♂; 266, *Bombycia algens* (Grote), ♂; 267, *Brachylomia discinigra* (Walker), ♀; 268, *Litholomia napaea* (Morrison), ♀; 269, *Lithomoia solidaginis* (Hübner), ♂.

Figs. 270–287. 270, *Xylena cineritia* (Grote), ♂; 271, *Lithophane tepida* Grote, ♀; 272 *L. lamda thaxteria* Grote, ♀; 273, *Lemmeria digitalis* (Grote), ♂; 274, *Mniotype versut* (Smith), ♀; 275, *Chaetaglaea sericea* (Morrison), ♀; 276, *Pyreferra citromba* Franclemont, ♀ 277, *Apamea plutonia* (Grote), ♂; 278, *A. inordinata* (Morrison), ♂; 279, *Lithophane semiust* Grote, ♂; 280, *L. patefacta* (Walker), ♂; 281, *L. bethunei* (Grote & Robinson), ♂; 282, *L. innominata* (Smith), ♂; 283, *L. petulca* Grote, ♂; 284, *L. petulca* Grote, ♂; 285, *L. amana* (Smith), ♂; 286, *L. disposita* Morrison, ♂; 287, *L. hemina* Grote, ♂.

Figs. 288–305. 288, *Lithophane grotei* Riley, ♂; 289, *L. baileyi* Grote, ♂; 290, *L. antennata* (Walker), ♂; 291, *L. georgii* Grote, ♂; 292, *L. laticinerea* Grote, ♀; 293, *L. oriunda* Grote, ♂; 294, *L. unimoda* (Lintner), ♀; 295, *L. fagina* Morrison, ♂; 296, *L. pexata* Grote, ♀; 297, *L. lepida* (Lintner), ♂; 298, *Xylena nupera* (Lintner), ♀; 299, *X. curvimacula* (Morrison), ♀; 300, *X. thoracica* (Putnam-Cramer), ♂; 301, *Xylotype acadia* Barnes & Benjamin, ♀; 302, *Platypolia anceps* (Stephens), ♂; 303, *Mniotype ducta* (Grote), ♀; 304, *M. miniota* (Smith), ♀; 305, *Fishia enthea* Grote, ♀.

Figs. 306–323. 306, *Sutyna privata* (Walker), ♂; 307, *S. profunda* (Smith), ♀; 308, *Psectraglaea carnosa* (Grote), ♀; 309, *Epiglaea decliva* (Grote), ♂; 310, *E. apiata* (Grote), ♀; 311, *Metaxaglaea inulta* (Grote), ♂; 312, *Pyreferra indirecta* (Walker), ♂; 313, *P. citromba* Franclemont, ♀; 314, *P. pettiti* (Grote), ♀; 315, *P. ceromatica* (Grote), ♀; 316, *Eupsilia tristigmata* (Grote), ♀; 317, *E. vinulenta* (Grote), ♀; 318, *E. morrisoni* (Grote), ♂; 319, *E. devia* (Grote), ♀; 320, *Parastichtis discivaria* (Walker), ♀; 321, *Sunira bicolorago* (Guenée), ♀; 322, *Xanthia lutea* (Ström), ♀; 323, *Anathix ralla* (Grote), ♀.

Figs. 324–341. 324, *Anathix puta* (Grote & Robinson), ♂; 325, *Eucirrhoedia pampina* (Guenée), ♂; 326, *Apamea apamiformis* (Guenée), ♀; 327, *A. verbascoides* (Guenée), ♀; 328, *A. nigrior* (Smith), ♀; 329, *A. cariosa* (Guenée), ♀; 330, *A. lignicolora* (Guenée), ♂; 331, *A. vultuosa* (Grote), ♂; 332, *Homoglaea hircina* Morrison, ♀; 333, *Apamea amputatrix* (Fitch), ♀; 334, *A. alia* (Guenée), ♂; 335, *A. indocilis* (Walker), ♂; 336, *A. impulsa* (Guenée), ♀; 337, *A. mixta* (Grote), ♀; 338, *A. commoda* (Walker), ♂; 339, *A. finitima* Guenée, ♀; 340, *Agroperina lateritia* (Hufnagel), ♂; 341, *A. dubitans* (Walker), ♂.

Figs. 342–359. 342, *Agroperina cogitata* (Smith), ♂; 343, *A. lutosa* (Andrews), ♀; 344, *A. helva* (Grote), ♂; 345, *Crymodes devastator* (Brace), ♂; 346, *Trichoplexia exornata* (Möschler), ♂; 347, *Protagrotis niveivenosa* (Grote), ♂; 348, *Luperina passer* (Guenée), ♂; 349, *Oligia modica* (Guenée), ♂; 350, *O. semicana* (Walker), ♂; 351, *O. bridghami* (Grote & Robinson), ♀; 352, *O. minuscula* (Morrison), ♂; 353, *O. diversicolor* (Morrison), ♂; 354, *O. illocata* (Walker), ♂; 355, *O. mactata* (Guenée), ♂; 356, *O. fractilinea* (Grote), ♂; 357, *Eremobina claudens* (Walker), ♀; 358, *E. jocasta* (Smith), ♀; 359, *Xylomoia chagnoni* Barnes & McDunnough, ♂.

Figs. 360–377. 360, *Spartiniphaga includens* (Walker), ♀; 361, *S. panatela* (Smith), ♀; 362, *Archanara subflava* (Grote), ♀; 363, *A. laeta* (Morrison), ♀; 364, *Hypocoena rufostrigata* (Packard), ♂; 365, *Senta defecta* Grote, ♀; 366, *Ipimorpha pleonectusa* Grote, ♂; 367, *Helotropha reniformis* (Grote), ♀; 368, *Amphipoea velata* (Walker), ♂; 369. *A. americana* (Speyer), ♀; 370, *A. interoceanica* (Smith), ♂; 371, *Hydroecia immanis* Guenée, ♂; 372, *H. stramentosa* Guenée, ♀; 373, *Papaipema cerina* (Grote), ♂; 374, *P. appassionata* (Harvey), ♂; 375, *P. inquaesita* (Grote & Robinson), ♂; 376, *P. marginidens* (Guenée), ♂; 377, *P. nepheleptena* (Dyar), ♂.

Figs. 378–395. 378, *Agroperina inficita* (Walker), ♀; 379, *Protagrotis extensa* (Smith), ♂; 380, *Luperina stipata* (Morrison), ♂; 381, *L. obtusa* (Smith), ♂; 382, *Oligia exhausta* (Smith), 383, *Archanara oblonga* (Grote), ♂; 384, *Hypocoena inquinata* (Guenée), ♀; 385, *Hydroecia micacea* (Esper), ♂; 386, *Papaipema duovata* (Bird), ♀; 387, *P. furcata* (Smith), ♂; 388, *P. arctivorens* Hampson, ♂; 389, *P. harrisii* (Grote), ♂; 390, *P. impecuniosa* (Grote), ♂; 391, *P. purpurifascia* (Grote & Robinson), ♀; 392, *P. lysimachiae* Bird, ♂; 393, *P. pterisii* Bird, ♀; 394, *P. cataphracta* (Grote), ♀; 395, *P. frigida* (Smith), ♂.

Figs. 396–413. 396, *Euplexia benesimilis* McDunnough, ♂; 397, *Phlogophora iris* Guenée, ♀; 398, *P. periculosa* Guenée, ♂; 399, *Conservula anodonta* (Guenée), ♂; 400, *Haploolophus mollissima* (Guenée), ♂; 401, *Euherrichia monetifera* (Guenée), ♀; 402, *Macronoctua onusta* Grote, ♂; 403, *Trachea delicata* (Grote), ♂; 404, *Chytonix palliatricula* (Guenée), ♂; 405, *C. sensilis* Grote, ♀; 406, *Cerma cora* Hübner, ♂; 407, *Leuconycta diphteroides* (Guenée), ♀; 408, *L. lepidula* (Grote), ♀; 409, *Agriopodes fallax* (Herrich-Shaeffer), ♀; 410, *A. teratophora* (Herrich-Shaeffer), ♀; 411, *Amphipyra pyramidoides* Guenée, ♀; 412, *A. tragopoginis* (Linnaeus), ♀; 413, *Dipterygia scabriuscula* (Linnaeus), ♀.

Figs. 414–431. 414, *Papaipema aweme* (Lyman), ♀; 415, *P. nelita* (Strecker), ♀; 416, *P. limpida* (Guenée), ♂; 417, *P. eupatorii* (Lyman), ♂; 418, *Fagitana littera* (Guenée), ♀; 419, *Polygrammate hebraeicum* Hübner, ♀; 420, *Amphipyra glabella* (Morrison), ♀; 421, *Andropolia contacta* (Walker), ♂; 422, *Platysenta sutor* (Guenée), ♀; 423, *Nedra ramosula* (Guenée), ♀; 424, *Hyppa xylinoides* (Guenée), ♂; 425, *Platysenta videns* (Guenée), ♂; 426, *P. vecors* (Guenée), ♀; 427, *Elaphria festivoides* (Guenée), ♂; 428, *Platyperigea multifera* (Walker), ♂; 429, *Crambodes talidiformis* (Guenée), ♂; 430, *Proxenus miranda* (Grote), ♂; 431, *P. mendosa* McDunnough, ♂.

Figs. 432–449.   432, *Galgula partita* Guenée, ♀ ; 433, *Balsa malana* (Fitch), ♀ ; 434, *Enargia infumata* (Grote), ♀ ; 435, *Balsa labecula* (Grote), ♂ ; 436, *Enargia decolor* (Walker), ♂ ; 437, *Spodoptera frugiperda* (J. E. Smith), ♂ ; 438, *Magusa orbifera* (Walker), ♀ ; 439, *Spodoptera ornithogalli* (Guenée), ♀ ; 440, *Balsa tristrigella* (Walker), ♂ ; 441, *Cosmia calami* (Harvey), ♂ ; 442, *Amolita fessa* Grote, ♂ ; 443, *Arzama obliqua* (Walker), ♂ ; 444, *Bellura diffusa* (Grote), ♀ ; 445, *Achatodes zeae* (Harris), ♀ ; 446, *Catabena lineolata* Walker, ♂ ; 447, *Ogdoconta cinereola* (Guenée), ♂ ; 448, *Eutricopis nexilis* Morrison, ♀ ; 449, *Pyrrhia umbra* (Hufnagel), ♂.

Figs. 450–484. 450, *Pyrrhia exprimens* (Walker), ♀ ; 451, *Helicoverpa zea* (Boddie), ♀ ; 452, *Schinia florida* (Guenée), ♀ ; 453, *S. trifascia* Hübner, ♂ ; 454, *S. obscurata* Strecker, ♂ ; 455, *Cryphia pervertens* Barnes & McDunnough, ♂ ; 456, *C. villificans* Barnes & McDunnough, ♂ ; 457, *Protocryphia secta* (Grote), ♀ ; 458, *Exyra rolandiana* Grote, ♂ ; 459, *Lithacodia bellicula* Hübner, ♂ ; 460, *L. muscosula* (Guenée), ♀ ; 461, *L. albidula* (Guenée), ♀ ; 462, *L. synochitis* (Grote & Robinson), ♀ ; 463, *L. concinnimacula* (Guenée), ♀ ; 464, *L. carneola* (Guenée), ♀ ; 465, *Elaphria versicolor* (Guenée), ♀ ; 466, *E. grata* Hübner, ♀ ; 467, *E. georgei* (Moore & Rawson), ♂ ; 468, *Amyna bullula* (Grote), ♂ ; 469, *Platyperigea meralis* (Morrison), ♂ ; 470, *Rhodoecia aurantiago* (Guenée), ♀ ; 471, *Heliothis phloxiphaga* Grote & Robinson, ♀ ; 472, *Neoerastria caduca* (Grote), ♂ ; 473, *Heliothis borealis* (Hampson), ♀ ; 474, *H. virescens* (Fabricius), ♀ ; 475, *H. paradoxa* (Grote), ♀ ; 476, *Schinia nundina* (Drury), ♂ ; 477, *S. arcigera* (Guenée), ♀ ; 478, *S. marginata* (Haworth), ♀ ; 479, *S. thoreaui* (Grote & Robinson), ♂ ; 480, *S. meadi* (Grote), ♂ ; 481, *Amyna octo* (Guenée), ♀ ; 482, *Tarachidia tortricina* (Zeller), ♀ ; 483, *Acontia aprica* (Hübner), ♀ ; 484, *Eutelia pulcherrima* (Grote), ♂.

Figs. 485–509. 485, *Neoerastria apicosa* (Haworth), ♀; 486, *Capis curvata* Grote, ♂; 487, *Chamyris cerintha* (Treitschke), ♂; 488, *Tarachidia erastrioides* (Guenée), ♀; 489, *T. candefacta* (Hübner), ♂; 490, *Acontia terminimaculata* (Grote), ♂; 491, *Marathyssa basalis* Walker, ♂; 492, *M. inficita* (Walker), ♀; 493, *Paectes oculatrix* (Guenée), ♀; 494, *Characoma nilotica* (Rogenhofer), ♀; 495, *Nycteola frigidana* (Walker), ♀; 496, *Baileya doubledayi* (Guenée), ♂; 497, *B. ophthalmica* (Guenée), ♂; 498, *B. dormitans* (Guenée), ♂; 499, *Caloplusia ignea similans* McDunnough, ♂; 500, *Syngrapha parilis* (Hübner), ♂; 501, *S. alticola* (Walker), ♀; 502, *S. microgamma montana* (Packard), ♀; 503, *S. diasema* (Boisduval), ♂; 504, *S. rectangula* (Kirby), ♀; 505, *S. alias* (Ottolengui), ♀; 506, *S. u-aureum* (Aurivillius), ♀; 507, *S. interrogationis* (Linnaeus), ♀; 508, *S. octoscripta* (Grote), ♀; 509, *S. surena* (Grote), ♂.

Figs. 510–527. 510, *Syngrapha epigaea* (Grote), ♂; 511, *S. selecta* (Walker), ♂; 512, *Anagrapha falcifera* (Kirby), ♀; 513, *Trichoplusia ni* (Hübner), ♂; 514, *Pseudoplusia oo* (Cramer), ♂; 515, *Chrysaspidia putnami* (Grote), ♂; 516, *C. contexta* (Grote), ♂; 517, *Autographa biloba* (Stephens), ♀; 518, *A. precationis* (Guenée), ♂; 519, *A. ampla* (Walker), ♂; 520, *A. sansoni* Dod, ♂; 521, *A. rubida* Ottolengui, ♂; 522, *A. bimaculata* (Stephens), ♂; 523, *A. mappa* (Grote & Robinson), ♂; 524, *A. pseudogamma* (Grote), ♂; 525, *A. flagellum* (Walker), ♀; 526, *Chrysanympha formosa* (Grote), ♂; 527, *Eosphoropteryx thyatyroides* (Guenée), ♀.

Figs. 528–543. 528, *Pseudeva purpurigera* (Walker), ♂; 529, *Plusia balluca* (Geyer), ♀; 530, *P. aereoides* (Grote), ♂; 531, *Allagrapha aerea* (Hübner), ♀; 532, *Abrostola urentis* Guenée, ♂; 533, *Catocala innubens* Guenée, ♀; 534, *C. epione* (Drury), ♀; 535, *Syngrapha altera* (Ottolengui), ♂; 536, *Trichoplusia oxygramma* (Geyer), ♂; 537, *Argyrogramma verruca* (Fabricius), ♀; 538, *Chrysaspidia venusta* (Walker), ♂; 539, *Parallelia bistriaris* Hübner, ♂; 540, *Euclidia cuspidea* (Hübner), ♂; 541, *Caenurgina crassiuscula* (Haworth), ♂; 542, *C. erechtea* (Cramer), ♂; 543, *Mocis latipes* (Guenée), ♂.

Figs. 544–561. 544, *Argyrostrotis anilis* (Drury), ♀; 545, *Zale lunata* (Drury), ♀; 546, *Z. unilineata* (Grote), ♀; 547, *Z. galbanata* (Morrison), ♀; 548, *Z. aeruginosa* (Guenée), ♀; 549, *Z. undularis* (Drury), ♀; 550, *Z. minerea* (Guenée), ♀; 551, *Z. lunifera* (Hübner), ♀; 552, *Z. submediana* McDunnough, ♀; 553, *Z. duplicata* (Bethune), ♀; 554, *Z. helata* (Smith), ♀; 555, *Z. horrida* Hübner, ♂; 556, *Panopoda rufimargo* (Hübner), ♂; 557, *P. carneicosta* Guenée, ♂; 558, *Cissusa spadix* (Cramer), ♂; 559, *Phoberia atomaris* Hübner, ♂; 560, *Synedoida grandirena* (Haworth), ♂; 561, *S. adumbrata alleni* (Grote), ♂.

Figs. 562–563. 562, *Erebus odora* (Linnaeus), ♂; 563, *Thysania zenobia* (Cramer), ♂.
Note: Figures 562 and 563 reproduced at 0.8 times natural size.

Figs. 564–577. 564, *Anticarsia gemmatalis* Hübner, ♀; 565, *Plusiodonta compressipalpis* Guenée, ♀; 566, *Strenoloma lunilinea* (Grote), ♀; 567, *Alabama argillacea* (Hübner), ♀; 568, *Calpe canadensis* Bethune, ♂; 569, *Anomis erosa* Hübner, ♀; 570, *Hypocala andremona* (Cramer), ♀; 571, *Scoliopteryx libatrix* (Linnaeus), ♀; 572, *Catocala antinympha* (Hübner) ♀; 573, *C. coelebs* Grote, ♀; 574, *C. habilis* Grote, ♂; 575, *C. serena* Edwards, ♀; 576 *C. mira* Grote, ♀; 577, *C. crataegi* Saunders, ♀.

Figs. 578–589. 578, *Catocala ultronia* (Hübner), ♀; 579, *C. coccinata* Grote, ♂; 580, *C. clintonii* Grote, ♀; 581, *C. blandula* Hulst, ♂; 582, *C. sordida* Grote, ♂; 583, *C. praeclara* Grote & Robinson, ♀; 584, *C. concumbens* Walker, ♂; 585, *Euparthenos nubilis* (Hübner), ♂; 586, *Catocala grynea* (Cramer), ♂; 587, *C. micronympha* Guenée, ♀; 588, *C. similis* Edwards, ♂; 589, *C. amica* (Hübner), ♂.

Figs. 590–592. *Catocala* spp. 590, *C. obscura* Strecker, ♂; 591, *C. residua* Grote, ♂; 592, *C. insolabilis* Guenée, ♂.

Figs. 593–595. *Catocala* spp. 593, *C. retecta* Grote, ♂; 594, *C. vidua* (J. E. Smith), ♀; 595, *C. piatrix* Grote, ♀.

Figs. 596–598. *Catocala* spp. 596, *C. palaeogama* Guenée, ♂; 597, *C. subnata* Grote, ♂; 598, *C. neogama* (J. E. Smith), ♀.

Figs. 599–601. *Catocala* spp. 599, *C. cerogama* Guenée, ♀; 600, *C. relicta* Walker, ♂; 601, *C. relicta* Walker, ♀.

Figs. 602–604. *Catocala* spp. 602, *C. amatrix* (Hübner), ♀; 603, *C. amatrix* (Hübner), ♂; 604, *C. cara* Guenée, ♂.

Figs. 605–607. *Catocala* spp. 605, *C. ilia* (Cramer), ♀; 606, *C. ilia* (Cramer), ♂; 607, *C. parta* Guenée, ♀.

Figs. 608–610. *Catocala* spp. 608, *C. briseis* Edwards, ♀; 609, *C. briseis* Edwards, ♀; 610, *C. meskei* Grote, ♂.

Figs. 611–613. *Catocala* spp. 611, *C. unijuga* Walker, ♂; 612, *C. semirelicta* Grote, ♀; 613, *C. innubens* Guenée, ♂.

INDEX TO GENERIC AND SPECIFIC NAMES

37	*Abagrotis*	92	*Amyna*
102	*Abrostola*	98	*Anagrapha*
61	*acadia*	35	*Anaplectoides*
36	*acadiensis*	45	*Anarta*
87	*Achatodes*	65	*Anathix*
93	*Acontia*	62	*anceps*
13	*Acronicta*	37	*anchocelioides*
12	*acronyctoides*	113	*andremona*
28	*Actebia*	10	*Androloma*
54	*Adita*	82	*Andropolia*
41	*adjuncta*	46	*Anepia*
113	*adumbrata alleni*	43	*anguina*
102	*aerea*	48	*Anhimella*
102	*aereoides*	109	*anilis*
110	*aeruginosa*	79	*anodonta*
19	*afflicta*	114	*Anomis*
81	*Agriopodes*	34	*Anomogyna*
69	*Agroperina*	59	*antennata*
26	*Agrotis*	113	*Anticarsia*
114	*Alabama*	103	*antinympha*
14	*albarufa*	66	*Apamea*
91	*albidula*	67	*apamiformis*
44	*albinuda*	54	*Apharetra*
21	*albipennis*	63	*apiata*
51	*Aletia*	92	*apicosa*
56	*algens*	35	*Aplectoides*
68	*alia*	75	*appassionata*
97	*alias*	93	*aprica*
102	*Allagrapha*	73	*Archanara*
97	*altera*	89	*arcigera*
37	*alternata*	76	*arctivorens*
96	*alticola*	114	*argillacea*
10	*Alypia*	99	*Argyrogramma*
58	*amanda*	109	*Argyrostrotis*
31	*Amathes*	38	*artesta*
106	*amatrix*	86	*Arzama*
13	*americana, Acronicta*	41	*assimilis*
74	*americana, Amphipoea*	53	*asteroides*
108	*amica*	46	*Astrapetis*
86	*Amolita*	28	*astricta*
74	*Amphipoea*	40	*atlantica*
81	*Amphipyra*	112	*atomaris*
100	*ampla*	34	*atrata*
67	*amputatrix*	37	*attenta*

87	*aurantiago*	102	*Catocala*
24	*aurulenta*	49	*Ceramica*
99	*Autographa*	29	*Cerastis*
78	*aweme*	75	*cerina*
		92	*cerintha*
32	*badinodis*	80	*Cerma*
54	*badistriga*	105	*cerogama*
95	*Baileya*	64	*ceromatica*
59	*baileyi*	63	*Chaetaglaea*
101	*balluca*	72	*chagnoni*
85	*Balsa*	92	*Chamyris*
94	*basalis*	94	*Characoma*
91	*bellicula*	12	*Charadra*
86	*Bellura*	30	*Chersotis*
79	*benesimilis*	24	*chimoensis*
58	*bethunei*	54	*chionanthi*
32	*bicarnea*	28	*Choephora*
65	*bicolorago*	101	*Chrysanympha*
99	*biloba*	99	*Chrysaspidia*
100	*bimaculata*	24	*churchillensis*
109	*bistriaris*	80	*Chytonix*
108	*blandula*	95	*cinereana*
56	*Bombycia*	87	*cinereola*
52	*borealis, Brachionycha*	61	*cineritia*
88	*borealis, Heliothis*	112	*Cissusa*
22	*bostoniensis*	64	*citromba*
52	*Brachionycha*	28	*clandestina*
56	*Brachylomia*	17	*clarescens*
71	*bridghami*	72	*claudens*
106	*briseis*	108	*clintonii*
36	*brunneicollis*	31	*c-nigrum*
92	*bullula*	107	*coccinata*
		103	*coelebs*
92	*caduca*	69	*cogitata*
109	*Caenurgina*	32	*collaris*
86	*calami*	11	*Colocasia*
96	*Caloplusia*	68	*commoda*
113	*Calpe*	51	*commoides*
22	*campestris*	113	*compressipalpis*
113	*canadensis*	55	*comstocki*
93	*candefacta*	91	*concinnimacula*
92	*Capis*	106	*concumbens*
46	*capsularis*	35	*condita*
106	*cara*	48	*confusa*
39	*carbonifera*	46	*congermana*
67	*cariosa*	15	*connecta*
112	*carneicosta*	79	*Conservula*
92	*carneola*	82	*contacta*
63	*carnosa*	99	*contexta*
87	*Catabena*	48	*contrahens*
77	*cataphracta*	53	*convexipennis*

56	*Copipanolis*
56	*Copivaleria*
80	*cora*
45	*cordigera*
86	*Cosmia*
84	*Crambodes*
109	*crassiuscula*
107	*crataegi*
47	*crenulata*
42	*cristifera*
49	*Crocigrapha*
70	*Crymodes*
90	*Cryphia*
36	*Cryptocala*
52	*Cucullia*
47	*culea*
37	*cupida*
38	*curialis*
92	*curvata*
61	*curvimacula*
109	*cuspidea*
47	*cynica*

13	*dactylina*
22	*declarata*
63	*decliva*
86	*decolor*
74	*defecta*
80	*delicata*
12	*deridens*
23	*detersa*
42	*detracta*
70	*devastator*
65	*devia*
31	*Diarsia*
96	*diasema*
86	*diffusa, Bellura*
50	*diffusa, Faronta*
57	*digitalis*
35	*dilucida*
81	*diphteroides*
82	*Dipterygia*
56	*discinigra*
65	*discivaria*
31	*dislocata*
58	*disposita*
24	*dissona*
48	*distincta*
25	*divergens*
71	*diversicolor*
48	*dolosa*

95	*dormitans*
95	*doubledayi*
26	*drewseni*
69	*dubitans*
62	*ducta*
78	*duovata*
111	*duplicata*

83	*Elaphria*
35	*elimata*
86	*Enargia*
62	*enthea*
101	*Eosphoropteryx*
98	*epigaea*
63	*Epiglaea*
103	*epione*
93	*erastrioides*
111	*Erebus*
109	*erechtea*
72	*Eremobina*
114	*erosa*
29	*Euagrotis*
66	*Eucirrhoedia*
109	*Euclidia*
36	*Eueretagrotis*
79	*Euherrichia*
108	*Euparthenos*
78	*eupatorii*
79	*Euplexia*
64	*Eupsilia*
28	*Eurois*
94	*Eutelia*
11	*Euthisanotia*
56	*Eutolype*
87	*Eutricopis*
21	*Euxoa*
48	*evicta*
71	*exhausta*
70	*exornata*
88	*exprimens*
70	*extensa*
91	*Exyra*

34	*fabulosa*
60	*fagina*
80	*Fagitana*
98	*falcifera*
81	*fallax*
50	*Faronta*
27	*Feltia*
28	*fennica*

55	*Feralia*	30	*haruspica*
86	*fessa*	16	*hasta*
83	*festivoides*	80	*hebraeicum*
68	*finitima*	111	*helata*
29	*fishii*	88	*Helicoverpa*
62	*Fishia*	88	*Heliothis*
101	*flagellum*	74	*Helotropha*
11	*flavicornis*	69	*helva*
52	*florea*	58	*hemina*
89	*florida*	30	*Hemipachnobia*
29	*forbesi*	20	*henrici*
101	*formosa*	31	*Heptagrotis*
72	*fractilinea*	27	*herilis*
17	*fragilis*	49	*hibisci*
12	*frater*	57	*Hillia*
78	*frigida*	66	*hircina*
95	*frigidana*	34	*homogena*
85	*frugiperda*	66	*Homoglaea*
22	*fumalis*	54	*Homohadena*
15	*funeralis*	47	*Homorthodes*
55	*funesta*	111	*horrida*
28	*fungorum*	75	*Hydroecia*
76	*furcata*	113	*Hypocala*
16	*furcifera*	73	*Hypocoena*
47	*furfurata*	82	*Hyppa*
110	*galbanata*	96	*ignea similans*
84	*Galgula*	105	*ilia*
113	*gemmatalis*	29	*illapsa*
28	*geniculata*	72	*illocata*
83	*georgei*	39	*imbrifera*
59	*georgii*	75	*immanis*
82	*glabella*	77	*impecuniosa*
26	*gladiaria*	35	*imperita*
42	*goodelli*	19	*impleta*
112	*grandirena*	44	*implicata*
39	*grandis*	19	*impressa*
30	*Graphiphora*	68	*impulsa*
83	*grata, Elaphria*	18	*inclara*
11	*grata, Euthisanotia*	73	*includens*
14	*grisea*	18	*increta*
60	*grotei, Lithophane*	64	*indirecta*
56	*grotei, Copivaleria*	68	*indocilis*
107	*grynea*	50	*inermis*
		69	*inficita, Agroperina*
103	*habilis*	94	*inficita, Marathyssa*
17	*haesitata*	54	*infixa*
18	*hamamelis*	86	*infumata*
79	*Haploolophus*	42	*ingravis*
76	*harrisii*	58	*innominata*
20	*Harrisimemna*	14	*innotata*

102	*innubens*	41	*lilacina*
68	*inordinata*	78	*limpida*
76	*inquaesita*	87	*lineolata*
74	*inquinata*	50	*linita*
104	*insolabilis*	91	*Lithacodia*
51	*insueta*	57	*Litholomia*
52	*intermedia*	57	*Lithomoia*
75	*interoceanica*	57	*Lithophane*
97	*interrogationis*	19	*lithospila*
16	*interrupta*	80	*littera*
63	*inulta*	30	*littoralis*
74	*Ipimorpha*	44	*lorea*
27	*ipsilon*	110	*lunata*
57	*iris, Hillia*	111	*lunifera*
79	*iris, Phlogophora*	113	*lunilinea*
		70	*Luperina*
27	*jaculifera*	43	*lustralis*
72	*jocasta*	65	*lutea*
55	*jocosa*	69	*lutosa*
31	*jucunda*	42	*lutra*
30	*juncta*	77	*lysimachiae*
		10	*mac-cullochi*
55	*kolthoffi*	80	*Macronoctua*
		72	*mactata*
85	*labecula*	85	*Magusa*
55	*labradoris*	55	*major*
43	*Lacinipolia*	85	*malana*
73	*laeta*	38	*Mamestra*
34	*laetabilis*	25	*manitobana*
15	*laetifica*	100	*mappa*
61	*lamda thaxteri*	94	*Marathyssa*
20	*lanceolaria*	89	*marginata*
11	*langtoni*	76	*marginidens*
54	*lapponica*	46	*maryx*
44	*Lasiestra*	90	*meadi*
44	*Lasionycta*	43	*meditata*
69	*lateritia*	54	*melaleuca*
39	*latex*	45	*melanopa*
60	*laticinerea*	84	*mendosa*
109	*latipes*	84	*meralis*
40	*legitima*	106	*meskei*
57	*Lemmeria*	25	*messoria*
38	*leomegra*	29	*Metalepsis*
60	*lepida*	63	*Metaxaglaea*
81	*lepidula*	75	*micacea*
13	*leporina*	96	*microgamma montana*
13	*lepusculina*	108	*micronympha*
50	*Leucania*	23	*mimallonis*
81	*Leuconycta*	110	*minerea*
114	*libatrix*	48	*minians*
67	*lignicolora*	62	*miniota*

71	*minuscula*	28	*occulta*
107	*mira*	23	*ochrogaster*
84	*miranda*	29	*Ochropleura*
68	*mixta*	93	*octo*
62	*Mniotype*	10	*octomaculata*
109	*Mocis*	97	*octoscripta*
46	*modesta*	94	*oculatrix*
17	*modica, Acronicta*	111	*odora*
71	*modica, Oligia*	87	*Ogdoconta*
26	*mollis*	33	*okakensis*
79	*mollissima*	71	*Oligia*
79	*monetifera*	44	*olivacea*
30	*monochromatea*	53	*omissa*
65	*morrisoni*	53	*Oncocnemis*
48	*Morrisonia*	22	*ontario*
16	*morula*	80	*onusta*
84	*multifera*	99	*oo*
51	*multilinea*	33	*opacifrons*
91	*muscosula*	95	*ophthalmica*
		85	*orbifera*
57	*napaea*	59	*oriunda*
82	*Nedra*	85	*ornithogalli*
78	*nelita*	47	*Orthodes*
92	*Neoerastria*	49	*Orthosia*
105	*neogama*	17	*ovata*
76	*nepheleptena*	47	*oviduca*
48	*Nephelodes*	51	*oxygala*
40	*nevadae*	98	*oxygramma*
87	*nexilis*		
98	*ni*		
66	*nigrior*	33	*Pachnobia*
94	*nilotica*	94	*Paectes*
38	*nimbosa*	104	*palaeogama*
70	*niveivenosa*	12	*pallescens*
19	*noctivaga*	80	*palliatricula*
49	*normani*	66	*pampina*
32	*normaniana*	73	*panatela*
108	*nubilis*	112	*Panopoda*
90	*nundina*	12	*Panthea*
61	*nupera*	75	*Papaipema*
95	*Nycteola*	30	*Paradiarsia*
		89	*paradoxa*
		109	*Parallelia*
21	*obeliscoides*	65	*Parastichtis*
20	*oblinita*	96	*parilis*
27	*obliqua, Agrotis*	105	*parta*
86	*obliqua, Arzama*	84	*partita*
73	*oblonga*	70	*passer*
103	*obscura, Catocala*	57	*patefacta*
43	*obscura, Polia*	26	*patula*
89	*obscurata*	36	*perattenta*
70	*obtusa*	79	*periculosa*

30	*Peridroma*	77	*pterisii*
25	*perpolita*	94	*pulcherrima*
34	*perquiritata*	41	*pulverulenta*
90	*pervertens*	54	*purpurea*
64	*pettiti*	77	*purpurifascia*
58	*petulca*	101	*purpurigera*
60	*pexata*	39	*purpurissata*
79	*Phlogophora*	66	*puta*
88	*phloxiphaga*	99	*putnami*
112	*Phoberia*	81	*pyramidoides*
44	*phoca*	64	*Pyreferra*
51	*phragmatidicola*	88	*Pyrrhia*
31	*phyllophora*		
102	*piatrix*	30	*quadrangula*
49	*picta*	15	*quadrata*
53	*piffardi*	23	*quebecensis*
84	*Platyperigea*		
62	*Platypolia*	14	*radcliffei*
82	*Platysenta*	40	*radix*
29	*plecta*	65	*ralla*
74	*pleonectusa*	82	*ramosula*
24	*pleuritica*	12	*Raphia*
101	*Plusia*	96	*rectangula*
49	*plusiaeformis*	21	*redimicula*
113	*Plusiodonta*	105	*relicta*
67	*plutonia*	74	*reniformis*
38	*Polia*	43	*renigera*
80	*Polygrammate*	104	*residua*
52	*postera*	18	*retardata*
107	*praeclara*	104	*retecta*
36	*prasina*	49	*revicta*
100	*precationis*	87	*Rhodoecia*
35	*pressus*	30	*Rhyacia*
62	*privata*	37	*Rhynchagrotis*
63	*profunda*	45	*richardsoni*
12	*propinquilinea*	25	*ridingsiana*
70	*Protagrotis*	53	*riparia*
90	*Protocryphia*	56	*rolandi*
36	*Protolampra*	91	*rolandiana*
47	*Protorthodes*	45	*rosea*
84	*Proxenus*	49	*rubescens*
16	*pruni*	100	*rubida*
56	*Psaphida*	31	*rubifera*
63	*Psectraglaea*	13	*rubricoma*
51	*Pseudaletia*	112	*rufimargo*
50	*pseudargyria*	36	*rufipectus*
101	*Pseudeva*	73	*rufostrigata*
101	*pseudogamma*	41	*rugosa*
99	*Pseudoplusia*		
31	*pseudorosaria freemani*	29	*salicarum*
47	*Pseudorthodes*	100	*sansoni*

37	*satyricus*	65	*Sunira*
30	*saucia*	15	*superans*
53	*saundersiana*	97	*surena*
82	*scabriuscula*	83	*sutor*
24	*scandens*	46	*sutrina*
89	*Schinia*	62	*Sutyna*
23	*scholastica*	54	*Sympistis*
114	*Scoliopteryx*	112	*Synedoida*
38	*Scotogramma*	96	*Syngrapha*
33	*scropulana*	91	*synochitis*
42	*secedens*		
90	*secta*		
40	*segregata*	40	*tacoma*
98	*selecta*	84	*talidiformis*
71	*semicana*	93	*Tarachidia*
106	*semirelicta*	33	*tecta*
57	*semiusta*	29	*tenebrifera*
80	*sensilis*	33	*tenuicula*
74	*Senta*	59	*tepida*
103	*serena*	81	*teratophora*
63	*sericea*	93	*terminimaculata*
21	*servita*	22	*tessellata*
45	*Sideridis*	56	*thaxteriana*
36	*sigmoides*	61	*thoracica*
46	*signata*	89	*thoreaui*
108	*similis*	101	*thyatyroides*
20	*Simyra*	112	*Thysania*
25	*sinelinea*	93	*tortricina*
32	*smithii*	80	*Trachea*
57	*solidaginis*	81	*tragopoginis*
107	*sordida*	38	*Tricholea*
112	*spadix*	46	*Tricholita*
28	*Spaelotis*	70	*Trichoplexia*
73	*Spartiniphaga*	98	*Trichoplusia*
34	*speciosa*	89	*trifascia*
19	*sperata*	38	*trifolii*
52	*speyeri*	20	*trisignata*
16	*spinigera*	64	*tristigmata*
85	*Spodoptera*	18	*tristis*
70	*stipata*	85	*tristrigella*
75	*stramentosa*	14	*tritona*
113	*Strenoloma*		
49	*Stretchia*	97	*u-aureum*
56	*styracis*	37	*Ufeus*
44	*subdita*	46	*Ulolonche*
73	*subflava*	107	*ultronia*
27	*subgothica*	88	*umbra*
39	*subjuncta*	110	*undularis*
111	*submediana*	45	*uniformis*
104	*subnata*	105	*unijuga*
18	*subochrea*	110	*unilineata*

60	*unimoda*	64	*vinulenta*
11	*unio*	88	*virescens*
51	*unipuncta*	27	*volubilis*
102	*urentis*	67	*vultuosa*
50	*ursula*		
		33	*wockei*
83	*vecors, Platysenta*		
47	*vecors, Pseudorthodes*	65	*Xanthia*
74	*velata*	32	*xanthographa*
23	*velleripennis*	61	*Xylena*
26	*venerabilis*	82	*xylinoides*
99	*venusta*	72	*Xylomoia*
66	*verbascoides*	48	*Xylomyges*
99	*verruca*	61	*Xylotype*
83	*versicolor*		
62	*versuta*	35	*youngii*
26	*vetusta*		
43	*vicina*	110	*Zale*
82	*videns*	88	*zea*
104	*vidua*	87	*zeae*
90	*villificans*	112	*zenobia*
15	*vinnula*		